Copyright © 2024 by Karren Urben

All rights reserved.

No portion of this book may be reproduced in any form without written permission from the publisher or author, except as permitted by U.K. copyright law.

Disclaimer

This book is solely about my own experiences and feelings it is not intended to sway anyone else in their opinions on anything or anyone. I have tried to recreate events and places from my own memories of them. In order to protect and maintain anonymity in some instances I have changed the names of individuals and of places. I have tried to follow the Covid-19 timeline and to explain the events only as I experienced or witnessed them. I apologise for any unintentional mistakes I may have made.

Book Cover by Karren Urben. The Book Cover image is from an oil painting of Termoli by ©Karren Urben

First edition 2024

Contents

Dedication	1
Acknowledgements	2
Foreword	3
1. The Fates align	5
2. Italy here we come	11
3. Lago di Como	15
4. Firenze - Florence	19
5. Gallery day.	26
6. All roads lead to Rome	29
7. Abruzzo	33
8. San Martino in Pensilis. Molise	38
9. Pompeii.	44
10. Positano	48
11. Vesuvius	53

12.	Final week in Abruzzo	57
13.	Heading for Home	66
14.	The world turns upside down.	71
15.	The land	78
16.	Hugs Galore	81
17.	August 2020	84
18.	Are we really going to do this?	91
19.	Emotional Rollercoaster	98
20.	Back to Italy	105
21.	Whirlwind.	107
22.	Land owners.	111
23.	A Brilliant Idea	114
24.	Broken	121
25.	Mad Dash	123
26.	On our way	126
27.	Italy	130
28.	Covid tests	133
29.	Home sweet home	138
30.	Pizza and Prosecco	141
Afterword		144

For our family:

Zoe, Cyrus, Phoenix, Niaz and Gigi
We are always under the same moon and you are all forever in our hearts and on our minds.

Acknowledgements

Also a big Thank you to all of you who have encouraged me to write. You know who you are !

And to Rosa, our Italian sister and our Italian Mamma, Maria without whom ......

Foreword

If you do not believe in a higher power that protects and directs us through life – the compelling story of Karren and Charlie Urben in this book is sure to test your faith in chance and coincidence.

There are too many fortuitous meetings, moments of pure serendipity, examples of divine timing and miraculous healing to conclude that the Urben's journey from Brighton, England to San Martino in Pensilis, Molise, Italy was merely good fortune.

In early 2024 I had the pleasure of interviewing Karren and Charlie on the '*I'm Moving to Italy!*' podcast from their villa perched on the edge of the Adriatic Sea surrounded by an olive grove and citrus trees with breathtaking views of the Tremiti Islands.

As they recounted their circuitous journey to their Italian Paradise every element and plot twist of their journey felt guided by the supernatural.

Not only will this book have you questioning everything you thought you believed about destiny but it is also the perfect book to read if you have been resisting chasing your own dreams.

As a wiser person than I once said "*A ship anchored in port cannot be guided by the winds of good fortune*"

Prepare to be inspired by this remarkable book that Karren Urben has poured her heart into. It will certainly give you the courage to pull up your anchors, unfurl your sails and begin moving towards the life that was meant for you.

As a fellow foreigner who moved to Italy, I am grateful to have Karren and Charlie as my Italian neighbours and consider myself blessed to count them as friends.

Nathan Heinrich

Founder of *All Roads Lead To Italy* & Host of the "*I'm Moving to Italy!*" podcast.

April 2024.

The Fates align

*C**hapter 1*

Never in a million years did I think that I'd up and live full time in a different country to our daughter.

We had, it's true, always wanted to buy a piece of land but the idea was for it to be in the UK. Whilst Charlie had had thoughts of us buying land abroad I didn't agree.

Many years ago whilst on holiday in France he had broached the subject. We had flown to Toulouse where we hired a car with no hard and fast plans beyond a start and finish place and date. It was a real adventure. We had a great time (perhaps that could be another story) but live there No, absolutely Not.

Which is what I said when he asked me

"But why wouldn't you live here?"

He'd asked me this as we drove for miles and miles, and yet more miles without a single glimpse of a person, a house or a town

"I need to know I can get to the UK quickly. I need to feel safe" was my panicked reply. I'm sure I'm not alone in having almost primeval feelings about places and situations, for example pine forests make me uneasy and now I realised being somewhere with no sign of habitation on the horizon in any which way made me feel positively uncomfortable.

So how and why did we come to live in the hilltop Comune of San Martino in Pensilis, just outside the town itself, in one of Italy's smallest and least known regions. And how is it that here we are both so content and happy not to mention feeling that we have found our own little spot of heaven.

It really begins with a knock on the door of our Brighton home seventeen years ago. I was expecting an Italian teacher to arrive to stay for three weeks so I opened the door with a wide smile that somehow got broader as Rosa Di Matteo smiled back. We hit it off immediately, like most important people who come into my life a gut reaction, a kind of 'oh, hallo, you're here' an expectancy that somewhere in your life journey this person will arrive.

The funny thing is, when looking back on it was that Rosa hadn't planned on coming with this particular group of students from the southern Italian town of Termoli and when she did step in at the last minute had originally been allocated a different lodging.

So the fates were aligned on that autumn morning in Brighton, England. Nothing about this stay with us, pleasant as it was, even allowing for the fact that Rosa's mum had also come to stay for part of the time, would have led either Charlie or me to believe we'd actually be living in her home town one day in the future, nor when I'd asked whereabouts in Italy she came from and she had replied "San Martino in Pensilis" did we have goosebumps. Or as I call it 'one of my tingles'

Fast forward to 2019.

Charlie and I had had a traumatic few years. He with a burst Duodenal Ulcer and loss of enormous amounts of blood. Followed by me with a stint in Intensive Care with Pneumonia and Sepsis. As if that wasn't enough a year later I was diagnosed with Ankylosing Spondilitis. It seemed our long held dream of buying a piece of land, creating a little campsite and Art Studio had disappeared in a puff of smoke.

There were of course the most wonderful highs the best of all being the birth of our first Grandchild Phoenix. She made everything brighter. When I came out of hospital I would drag myself up to a sitting position and read her piles of story books and when she and Zoe left I'd literally collapse in a heap. Charlie and Zoe stopped telling me off for doing this when I explained that not only was it THE highlight of my day but that I was determined she would never think of me as her poor old Granny sitting in the corner but would remember a huge welcoming smile and all the love in the world beaming out on her.

I always remember my own Grandmother's arms open wide as she stood at her front door with a big smile when we visited them. After her warm hug I would dash into the sitting room and leap onto my Grandad's lap into his loving safe arms. These memories have stayed with me all my life and are the happiest memories from a very dysfunctional unhappy childhood.

Which is probably why for me it's so important that my five , that is Zoe, her husband Cyrus, Phoenix, Niaz and Gigi not only know how loved they are but actually feel it.

And then there were terrible lows when one of my best friends died in 2018. I still miss her. Only the other day something happened and I thought of how much I wanted to discuss it with her. Here though is another strange thing when I look back on it. When LouLou was dying I wanted to fly out to Greece where she lived, and be with her and her Mum but being Christmas the only flights available involved changes and took such a long time that it was very clear to Charlie and me that by the time I reached Athens I would have been in a bad way. I just wasn't strong enough to do it. As anyone can imagine my thoughts were with her and her family all the time and I was getting into a bit of a state berating myself for not being able to be with her when I came across a language App which was offering a free trial. I just started clicking away at it and found myself immersed. I had picked Italian as the language to learn, no doubt inspired by a trip that Zoe and I had taken to Rome. Whilst I was taking the first steps of learning Italian I couldn't obsess over what was happening in Athens. Then I just kept going and subscribed for a year .

Then there was the loss of my Daisy. Daisy was our first West Highland Terrier. She came into my life the day that Rosa had left to go back to Italy after that first auspicious meeting. She and I were inseparable and her loyalty was boundless. When I came out of hospital she lay on my feet and refused to go anywhere other than a quick pee in the garden....(her ashes are here with us in Italy),

Another blow had been the decline of Charlie's Mum Doreen's health. A strong woman with a vibrant personality Mum was fiercely independent, she had loved to travel, had been a keen and very good ballroom dancer but now as physical frailty curtailed her so dementia started to set in. There wasn't any way we could have her to live with us, simply because Pace and Rest is the mantra I have to live by to keep me healthy, so the next best thing was THE best place she could afford. We found it in Henfield and it was expensive but she had a lovely room, beautiful grounds and most importantly stimulation and we strongly felt that by the time the money ran out she wouldn't then be aware of where she was, but all the time she was still fully aware, it was very important to all of us as a family that she was comfortable and happy.

We had some joyous times there too. For example on her birthday the Home arranged for us to use a lovely big room, they laid out a tea party and we all went Sue, her partner and her children. Zoe and Cyrus and a couple of Doreen's friends it was lovely.

By 2019 my A.S was under control although not cured as it is a chronic and progressive form of Arthritis, it had taken a long time but with medication, exercise and good old 'Pace and Rest'. However by using these tools I was now able to walk without using sticks I was doing regular hydrotherapy and was once again at my easel painting.

Life however was much smaller and slower I was still in pain and even worse was the fatigue.

We'd moved from Brighton to a little seaside village called Ferring. It's a very pretty village with a slower pace of life and most important for us it was flat. That meant I could walk daily without causing Flare up's and was the prime reason for the move. The second reason being that I was unable, at that time to walk up or down the stairs without intense pain. It had felt a wrench leaving Brighton with Zoe being nearby but health wise it was the best thing to do. I was able to drive the five minutes to the beach and walk the dogs on the sand or, when the tide was high the dogs and I would stroll along the Tamarisk lined pathway to the Bluebird Cafe. The skies there are huge, when the sea recedes there are vast swathes of sand unlike Brightons pebbles, and often virtually empty of humans. Populated instead by a variety of seabirds including my favourites, the Oystercatchers. On a clear day it is even possible to see the Isle of Wight. Daisy and Archie, and later, Archie and Betsy along with their Westie cousin Maisie Grey (when she came to stay) would run and run. Their big Westie smiles all over their faces, chasing each other or the flocks of gulls, causing the birds to lift off in unison like a large blanket being shaken up in the air.

Around this time we decided to take out an Equity Release on our house. We were property rich and cash poor. Charlie working all the hours possible and I was unable to do an awful lot to contribute.

Equity Release meant we could pay off the mortgage giving Charlie less pressure. We would be able to take a long holiday in the Fifth Wheel Caravan (Which was named LouLou Bella. It was so called because she had planned to get a little motorhome but as that never transpired we decided to name our van after her). We also planned a much desired trip to Rome.

My first visit to Rome was in 2009. Zoe took me for a City break for my birthday. An amazing gift from an amazing daughter.

I fell in love with the City and just knew that Charlie would too. He did. We spent Easter 2019 there and it was amazing.

If you've never been before and have a love of history it is just incredible. Every corner of the Borgo Antico whispers to you from the ancient past.

So, with all the treatment, medication and exercise I'd slowly got stronger and eventually was able to book myself a One Woman Exhibition at Colonnade House in Worthing. This was a huge milestone. Even if I hadn't had the sales that I did it would still have been an enormous success in my mind as the mere fact that I was able to put this collection of work together after everything that had happened was a huge achievement.

Of course Charlie and I never do things by half so not content with putting on a Solo show we'd also booked a ferry and were off to Italy to visit my brother and his wife, to have that long holiday... the day after we broke the exhibition down.

Italy here we come

Chapter 2

It didn't get off to the greatest of starts.

We were woken very early that morning by a loud banging on the front door and the dogs were going doolally. Jumping out of bed we opened the front door to Charlie's Mitsubishi truck on fire. Our neighbours were leaving for work and had spotted the smoke, woken us and called the fire brigade so thankfully it was soon under control.

Our immediate thought after knowing the fire was out and no one hurt was Thank God it wasn't the other pickup as the Dodge Ram would be pulling the Fifth Wheel caravan to Italy and our holiday would have gone up in smoke along with the truck.

When we did eventually pull away, it was just after the wrecking vehicle had loaded up the burnt out Mitsubishi so it was with a huge sigh of relief that we got on the road towards Dover where we had booked a campsite.

The following morning we would be on the Ferry to Calais.

It's always a wonderful feeling leaving for any kind of holiday. If you are a motor-homer / caravaner you'll understand when I say the head count was done, the passports, cards, cash, phones and the chargers were all in one place and you can breathe because the beauty of this kind of holiday is simply that you know you have everything you need for every eventuality of weather. You are guaranteed decent coffee first thing in the morning and, if you've done your homework a good view to gaze at while you sip it.

We set off that morning with no clue that this trip was going to be an absolute life changer. We had no reason to. The Equity release had paid off our mortgage enabling Charlie to take the whole month off work. I was painting again and had had the successful Solo exhibition. The kids were all well and happy. Mum was in good hands. And, we were content. We liked our house in Ferring and all our dreams of buying land were in the past we'd accepted it wasn't going to be.

So off we set our thoughts were only of an adventurous drive down to Central Italy, visit David and Ann followed by a slow meander back through France and home in time to enjoy the Christmas preparations.

Little did we know.

We congratulated ourselves on booking the pitch at Dover it gave us breathing space to at least partially unwind before embarking on the holiday proper. I was still on a high at having got the Exhibition together. Memories of the Private View were even now giving me an internal warm hug of appreciation for the family, friends and supporters who came but it had also been exhausting because at the same time I had been packing up the van whenever I had a spare moment. Now I was able to put my feet up not just physically but also mentally.

We have always divided our work load playing to our own strengths. Charlie, alongside his own work had been preparing the Ram and the Van all those things that were needed to be ready. Meanwhile I had packed up the internal making sure we had clothes for the warmer climes of Central Italy alongside the autumn and early winter weather of northern Europe. Snow-chains had to be onboard because by November it's law and we would be returning across the mountains then.

Being at the site in Dover we slowly unwound. We walked Betsy and Archie then sat with a Marks and Spencer meal deal sipped the wine and chatted about the last few hectic weeks. The shock of the other truck catching fire had barely sunk in.

By the time we got into bed we were feeling a lot more relaxed I'd had a potter around inside, repacking a few things and Charlie has done the same outside the van, double checking all was ready for the long journey ahead.

We were up early the next morning made a pot of coffee, walked the dogs then we were off. The skies were blue and the sea calm we sat up on deck and watched the white cliff's of Dover recede before going down to the restaurant for some breakfast. Charlie had been anxious about how it would go taking the fifth wheel on the ferry. Our previous van journeys abroad had been in a motorhome so he had been relieved as we were directed in alongside the HGV's and all had gone well and smoothly.

The dogs had slept comfortably on the front seats as we discovered when we returned to the vehicle as the ferry sailed into the harbour.

Disembarking at Calais we were soon on the road, we'd decided to drive through Belgium taking the route David had told us about. Our first night we stayed at a charming little site in Arlon, Belgium which is close to the border of Luxembourg. I remember it being quite cold in the evening because when we stepped into the little restaurant on site we were greeted with a blast of warm air from their wood burner. It was very friendly and the food was good. Betsy and Archie were happy too as they were welcomed in to lay at our feet.

Oh, and the loo's were fun. The wall's in the Ladies were covered in pictures of Paris, a variety of perfume bottles adorned the shelves while the music of Charles Aznavour piped through, it was quite an experience. Charlie told me that the Men's had pictures of New York on their walls and the piped music was Frank Sinatra.

The next morning we set off for Germany where we had booked a campsite for one night unfortunately they hadn't taken into account our height so we had to go to another place when it became apparent that we couldn't drive underneath the arched wall at the entrance. This was called Kaiser Camping and was nice enough but as we were leaving the following morning I slammed my own thumb in the truck door and OMG did it hurt, a Dodge Ram door is HEAVY. The nice guy at reception gave me some ice in a tea-towel as I'd been going in to pay. So it was with a swollen and throbbing thumb that we went into Switzerland and then approached the Gotthard Tunnel.

Lago di Como

Chapter 3

"Come on, come with me" Charlie was standing in the open doorway with his hand out stretched.

I was tired and very grumpy.

It had been a hell of a day and we were both exhausted all I wanted to do was eat and go to sleep. While I started to prepare something to eat he had taken the dogs for a walk and now was asking me to join him.

I can't resist him when he smiles like that so I agreed, still somewhat of a grump to be fair and followed him out and along the path. The campsite was very quiet we'd booked in for the very last night of the season. There was a gateway at the end of the path. Pushing it open we stepped out to see Lake Como before us glistening under the moon. It was magical.

We sat on a bench holding hands just gazing out as lights were flickering on, on the opposite shore, up in the hills and away to the left then to the right the reflections dancing on the still water.

It was so beautiful.

We sat until we felt too cold to sit any longer then turned back to the campsite gate but first I tugged at Charlies hand pulled him in for a kiss and said Thank you.

The day, as I said earlier had started with my thumb being painfully shut in the door, and the journey was pretty uneventful and rather boring to start with.

I don't think I've mentioned that I'm not someone who particularly enjoys the actual journey, I mean sometimes yes but I don't like sitting about for too long as I get kind of restless and want to be doing something and we had now been in the van for 4 days. But as the miles were eaten up and we neared the Italian border I was getting more interested in the journey itself. The trouble is that when you, well ok, that is when I, read a map, I forget about the mountain bit. The up hill and down dale, or more of 'up the precipice and down again' so the road to Lake Como took much longer than we'd initially thought, however we were now in Italy and the scenery was beautiful (when, that is we weren't going through the many tunnels) but truth be told by the time we got close to the Lake we were both tired and hungry and the other thing that neither of us had taken into account was the fact that unless you take the main road into Como and around the lake you will be driving on very narrow, extremely winding roads and there we were in a long truck which was towing an even longer fifth wheel caravan.

I was gazing out of the window catching glimpses of the lake through the tree's I was trying to avoid looking down as I have an aversion to heights and we did seem to be very close to the edge. The Ram is a left hand drive and it felt as though I was actually hanging over a precipice, so my gaze was directed determinedly across the water when I heard a loud expletive from Charlie and turning my head saw with horror why. There in front of us on a narrow bend was a huge coach bearing up towards us showing, or so it seemed no sign of stopping. I guess the driver was used to idiot tourists like us because stop he eventually did and very patiently waited while Charlie backed up. Fortunately we had started using walkie talkies a few years back when we'd purchased our first long motorhome. These enabled us to safely maintain contact whilst out of actual view of each other in the wing mirrors. We were very grateful for them now as I got out to guide Charlie back. There was, of course, a queue of cars who also had to back up. I was rather embarrassed especially as I was travelling in a very comfy extremely unflattering pair of joggers, rolled down sheepskin boots and a baggy probably slightly grubby top. Whilst this kind of outfit looks fabulous on some people I knew it didn't on me, but hey what was I doing even thinking about that when there were more important things to think about it. Thankfully no one was shouting at me, and maybe there were one or two toots of the horn but nothing aggressive I just kept smiling rather manically and eventually Charlie, omg my hero, backed into a kind of lay by and the bus passed on by with the passengers waving out of the windows.

Eventually and heaving huge sighs of relief we came to the road where the campsite was situated. We drove along the lane feeling considerably more cheerful with visions of putting our feet up with glasses of wine hovering in front of us. Charlie stopped the truck just before the right hand turning and out I got to make sure it was the right place.

The lady at the reception greeted me warmly and thankfully spoke English, yes I had been using the language App but learning by rote and faced with listening, comprehending and responding to anything other than Buon giorno or Ciao seemed unlikely. Motioning to Charlie that we had the right place he started to turn into the road then we realised we had a problem. It was too tight Way too tight. We had a silent onlooker up on the balcony of the house that Charlie was trying to avoid scraping or, worse. Eventually I went back to reception, this was where I was completely thankful for her English as after I had explained the situation she called her son who came out jumped into his car and led us up onto the main road. A very busy road it was too. Undeterred he promptly stopped all the traffic so that we could back all the way up it was a Deja Vu moment for sure. Once Charlie had backed up far enough he was able to turn right and drive back down to the little turn off for the campsite which this time with a left hand turn we managed to do.

So by the time we had checked in and gone through the rigamarole of getting ourselves onto a rather tight pitch we were both understandably exhausted and I was grumpy which was when Charlie had returned from the shortest dog walk in history and said

" Come on. Come with me".

Firenze - Florence

*C*hapter 4

The next morning we made coffee and taking our mugs with us went back to the same bench as the evening before. It was so beautiful and so tranquil.

The perfect start to our first full day in Italy.

We managed to get ourselves off the pitch, out of the campsite and turn up onto the main road with no problems at all. Passing through little towns or villages set beside the lake we got glimpses of the water then we were heading over the bridge as we set off towards Milan onto the Autostrada to Bologna where it was foggy and chilly.

Florence was our destination, the City Camp site to be precise which is set beside the River Arno.

I was eager to get there. As I've previously mentioned we both enjoy history on top of which I'm a bit of a bookworm and while I could never claim to be any kind of expert I was really looking forward to being able to walk the streets of Florence for the first time, to stroll where amongst many illustrious others The Medici's and Michelangelo had done so all those years ago.

The scenery was picturesque with Tuscany's green hill's undulating before us pretty villa's dotted here and there with clusters of cypress trees. Before long we were slowly descending and coming into the city. After our experience the day before we couldn't quite believe how easy it was to find the site with an added bonus that it had a wide entrance and a spacious area for parking. We checked in with our wide smiles faltering only slightly as it turned out we had to pay for two pitches because of our size, regardless of the fact we'd booked and filled in all the details but hey ho we were on holiday and there was nothing to be done about it so we took it on the chin got back into the truck and went to find our pitch. On finding our spot we were dismayed to see how tight it was even having two of them side by side. To say there was a lot of shunting going on is an understatement plus we had an audience. In fact so much to'ing and fro'ing was needed to get into the space that I began to feel sea sick.

Charlie's mutterings were getting louder and a darker shade of blue until eventually we were tucked into our allocated space able to unhitch the truck and get the slide out extended. Betsy and Archie were soon happily sniffing and marking out their territory on their staked leads. As soon as the gas was on I made a cup of tea. Charlie bless him needed a cold beer after all the parking shenanigans.

It was such a relief to know we now had three nights here in Florence and for the first time since we'd left I was able to get things out of cupboards and make things nice. It's always been important to me to make wherever I am cosy and comfortable warm and welcoming. Charlie laughs at me sometimes but he likes it really.

The dogs needed to stretch their legs and we were looking forward to exploring. It was a big site with not only travelling pitches but also static vans and little cabins. At the entrance was a Restaurant and Bar with a large outdoor seating area overlooking the swimming pool which had quite a few people splashing around in it. Intrigued by the huge pipework we discovered they brewed their own beer so obviously it would have been rude not to try it, at least that was what Charlie told me. If I was going to add emoji's I'd be putting in the laughing face.

From the entrance a wide thoroughfare led us though the various habitation area's, past shower blocks and to a gate, passing through which and, with both dog's pulling us, their noses eagerly twitching, we found ourselves on the bank of the River Arno.

They were ecstatic they were able to run off the leads for the first time since leaving home. We wandered more sedately behind them drinking in our surroundings. The reflections playing on the water were in yellow ochres, terracottas and pale greens from the buildings that stood in front of a gracefully curved Weir . We followed the waters path to our right as it splashed over the staggered steps and on towards the historic centre of Florence itself.

The following morning we were woken by a bugle, it sounded like a Reveille. Somewhere not too far away perhaps there was some kind of camp. Groaning and glancing at phones we realised that all four of us had slept in until 8.00. Feeling grateful for such a civilised hour for an alarm call we clambered out of bed.

We walked over to the restaurant where we sat in the warm sunshine with fresh croissants and coffee before getting on the courtesy shuttle bus and heading over to the city itself.

The bus stopped just by one of the bridges that cross the river from there it looped back to the site. From the stop it's a pleasant walk along the bank before crossing another bridge from which we took lots of photos of the Ponte Vecchio and then you're there on the edge of the historic city.

We loved it.

It has a sense of intimacy that other cities don't have, maybe in part because of the narrow streets and alleyways. I am writing this a few years later and memory can be picky but that's the feeling I retain and Charlie remembers it in the same way. It didn't feel hurried and although there were tourists, not as many as there would be in the height of the summer. We explored the streets, peering in through the dusty windows of an Atelier where various sculptures appeared to be in process of being restored.

Popping into Zecchi the famous Art Supply shop I drooled over the oil paint selection and treated myself to a Zecchi Artists smock.

We marvelled at the Duomo and St. Johns Basilica and strolled through the Piazza della Signoria with it's replica of the statue of David. Our intention was simply to wander around, to really drink in the atmosphere also the fact that we had the dogs with us meant we wouldn't be able to visit any of the Galleries which in a way is freeing because when you know you can just wander and just be, you get to see and appreciate more of the little things whereas when there is a timetable to adhere to it can get a little rushed.

At lunch time we didn't have a clue where to go but knew we didn't want to go anywhere touristy so while I was purchasing a gorgeous Medici handbag (my birthday present from Charlie) I asked the shop owner if he would recommend a place where the locals ate.

"L'Oste is where I eat my lunch every day" he said and gave us directions, so we set off to find it and were fortunate to get a table.

As highly as I recommend it to meat eaters it is perhaps not the best choice if you have vegetarians in your party. On entering you come face to face with glazed floor to ceiling fridges where you see just how fresh your meal will be. Even meat eaters may not appreciate this sight, of course forewarned you can now avert your gaze. I was certainly glad that our table was in a room away from them. The food was mouthwateringly delicious. The restaurant also had a great atmosphere. Bustling although not hectic it was friendly despite being so busy. We now recommend it to anyone we know thats going to Florence.

Betsy and Archie lay under the table salivating, being remarkably well behaved. They were rewarded later as the portions of steak were not only tender and tasty but enormous and the doggy bags we left with meant they ate slices of steak with their meals for a couple of days.

We had had such a wonderful day. It was truly magical.

I was, I think on cloud nine from being on the very stones and cobbles that all those historical character's had trodden, in the centuries past.

When Zoe and I were in Rome in 2009 I had stood at the Temple of the Vestal Virgins and cried.

Zoe was bewildered " Mum. Are you crying ! OMG".

I tried to explain that as a girl of thirteen I'd read about the Vestal Virgin's for the first time and back then would never have dreamt that one day I would actually be standing at the very temple.

I still get totally immersed in books so when I visit places like Florence or Rome its just amazing to me on so many levels.

Charlie and I then wandered over the Ponte Vecchio. This is something I would love to do very early in the morning before it becomes crowded with tourists and hawkers. I saw enough to want to go back but not nearly enough as it was so full of people.

Heading back to the bus stop our feet were aching and as we were both in need of the loo we decided to sit and have a coffee. There was a restaurant ahead in a great position overlooking the river, pulling out two chairs we sank into them in relief.

Betsy and Archie lay under the table. A waiter came with a menu then Charlie went to the loo. I waited for the guy to return to take the order and was still waiting when Charlie returned. Then it was my turn to find the loo's.

The bathroom was a mess, none too clean, a wet floor and no soap but I was grateful regardless.

Back to the table. We sat and waited. And waited.

We must have been there for half an hour at least, the lunch time rush was well and truly over so it's not as though we were being impatient, we were just being either ignored or forgotten. The couple next to us had had their order taken and had sat down at the same time. Deciding we'd waited long enough we got up and walked along the road towards the bus stop when we heard shouting behind us.

Turning we saw a man running towards us his face red with exertion screaming, shouting and waving his arms. We couldn't understand who he was chasing as turning our heads this way and that we couldn't see anyone running …Oh was he shouting at us?

He was. It turned out that he was the owner of the restaurant and was furious that we'd used the bathroom and not ordered anything. We in turn felt most indignant after all we'd sat there waiting to order coffees for at the very least half an hour. He was demanding a euro each for using his facilities. I felt furious at the unfairness of it but disinclined to argue over 2 euro's.

We felt even more annoyed when he said how fed up he was with tourists just coming to Florence to use his bathroom!

I cannot tell you how frustrated I felt as I fumbled in my bag for the coins. We were in the middle of a busy street with everyone staring at us unable to explain our point of view in Italian.

If that wasn't an incentive to re double my Italian language efforts I don't know what was. I hate unfairness and it bothered me that he assumed we were that kind of tourist. Now looking back I think that he was very likely at the end of his tether after a long season, but even so I would like to have been able to tell him that the least we should have had, for the price of a euro each was a clean loo and some soap.

Gallery day.

Chapter 5

Late afternoon of that same day saw me sitting on the river bank with my easel. A perfect way to relax after the busy morning. I love to paint Plein air and this was my first opportunity to get my easel and oil paints out. What a delicious spot it was too. Warm and sunny with the sound of birds and the water tumbling over the weir to keep me company.

Charlie relaxed back at the van with his book and a cold beer.

He brought the dogs over to see me after an hour or so. I was glad when he did as I was torn between continuing to paint or pack up because my ankles were bitten to pieces. I was sitting in long grass not the best place to choose and every time I thought I really must stop I'd see something else that I wanted to adjust or add, so by the time he arrived my ankles were pretty well covered in itchy red blotches. It was definitely time to call it a day.

Betsy and Archie were of course delighted to have another run along the riverbank so while I was packing up my equipment Charlie wandered along with them.

The following day was for me Gallery Day. I had booked tickets for the Galleria dell'Accademia for a morning tour and for the Uffizi Gallery in the afternoon.

It's always a mixed bag when you have your fur babies on holiday with you. Italy in general is a brilliant destination for a dog friendly holiday as most places allow them in, however there are some places where that is not possible and understandably so.

Now, Charlie is not averse to Galleries, we've wandered happily around quite a number together but he was equally happy to relax while I went off on my Art immersion day.

I took the courtesy bus then once again found myself strolling along the bank of the broad Arno River admiring the reflections on the water. It felt good to know where I was going, to be able to relax and gaze all around because now I was following in yesterdays footsteps.

I had plenty of time and had decided to head for the same coffee shop that we'd visited the day before the Kaleo Art Cafe in Duomo Piazza. A people watchers paradise as well as friendly with great coffee.

The Accademia tour was led by a guide who got rather impatient with other groups whose own guides were perhaps rushing along and tangling up with us. He was very funny about it too and had our group quietly laughing at his antics. He was obviously passionate about the Gallery and the works of art within and he made the tour all the more valuable for his passion.

Then there was 'David'. He gazes down from his plinth under a domed skylight the white marble gleaming. Seventeen feet (5.17 metres) tall he is truly remarkable. A real Wow moment when you see him here in all his glory.

If you ever debate whether or not it's worth going in to see the original, after all viewing the replica in the Piazza della Signoria is free, I would say, if you have the time and the budget then absolutely do. You not only get to gaze upon this real treasure but it's placed in such a way that you are able to walk around him admiring each and every angle. The light is perfect highlighting the beauty of his strongly muscled limbs.

After a panini back at the Kaleo cafe I mooched around before heading to the Piazza della Signoria where I perched on the steps of the Loggia Dei Lanzi. It seemed the spot to sit as many others were doing the same thing. I got out my little sketchbook to wait until it was time to meet the group for the Uffizi tour. It had rained and the square glistened, the sketches were just scribbles but I was enjoying just being there. I was sitting sketching in a square in Florence !

Oh it was a happy moment.

The Uffizi is wonderful. The paintings are of course breathtaking. So many Masterpieces, and the colours are so fresh, rich and stunning. The guide here too was passionate about the work and about Florence. It's an amazing building and also displays a large collection of ancient statues and busts from the Medici family. It is, in my opinion an absolute must for the 'to visit' list.

I floated back to the campsite and that evening as we ate delicious wood fired pizza at the on site restaurant I wittered on endlessly about my day while Charlie enjoyed a pint or two of the delicious larger they brew.

Whether he was really listening, or just making the right noises at the right time I don't know but we had a lovely last evening in Florence and soon started discussing the route for the following day.

All roads lead to Rome

*C*hapter 6

And we were off. Florence had been amazing and now I was looking forward to seeing my brother and where he now lived.

We headed towards Rome on the A1 before turning across the mountains towards the seaside city of Pescara which sits on the Adriatic coastline.

It was very green and beautiful with little towns dotted high up all around us. Being so far up we saw lots of buzzards and hawks, we may even have seen eagles but I wouldn't know as when I try to use binoculars in a moving vehicle I end up feeling car sick and frustrated. My (non fiction) audio book of choice on this leg of the journey was about Caterina Sforza Lady of Imola and Countess of Forli. Caterina a strong ruler stood her ground against the Borgia Popes army led by Cesare Borgia. It felt so apt as here we were travelling roads that the

Roman armies had more than likely used themselves and many of the hill towns looked, from the distance of the road as though they hadn't changed very much in all that time.

Pescara is the largest City in Abruzzo. It is situated right on the coast. With its beautiful beaches and modern shopping areas it attracts a large influx of tourists each summer.

Just before reaching the city itself we took a right turn towards our meeting point with David and Ann . The Adriatic Sea was now sparkling on our left all the way along creating that jolly holiday feeling.

They had arranged to meet us at the end of our turn off from the road from Pescara having explained that finding their place could be difficult.

We were very grateful for their consideration as quite frankly the thought of another hair raising, reversing up a hill, kind of episode was not appealing.

We came through the Toll and there they both were. It was so good to see them we jumped out for quick hugs before clambered back in and followed them. The way to Casalanguida is fine once you've done it at least once but I was very glad we weren't doing it alone that first time as I am pretty sure the Sat Nav would have sent us here there and everywhere and some of those roads are very twisty.

Abruzzo is a beautiful region of Italy and the area we were now in was full of vines and olive groves. Towns graced the top of the hills. Their terracotta rooftops and church spires catching the sun as it slowly dropped in the sky.

Every now and then we saw a large bird of prey fly across green fields, vines and olive trees. Then, it all changed suddenly to a parched yellow vista which seemed a stark contrast to seconds before. These may have been vast swathes of stubble after the harvest I'm not sure but it was strangely beautiful with its backdrop of the sea.

David and Anns house, Casa Mae sits at the end of a long driveway and was glowing in the setting sun. It's yellow walls lit up in warmth and welcome. After Charlie had manoeuvred up the drive with David and I calling out directions we got in through the gates and into position. Meanwhile Ann had been preparing the evenings Aperitivo.

The Italians have this wonderful custom which is the Aperitivo. Possibly, it's the equivalent of the Happy Hour. The difference being this - Happy Hour is often an opportunity to down as much alcohol as humanly possible at a cheaper price whereas the Aperitivo is a civilised laid back occasion to meet up with friends before dinner, to enjoy a drink, not even necessarily alcoholic, along with some snacks to stimulate the appetite for the evening meal. Sometimes the snacks are just a little bowl of nuts or crisps whilst at other times a smorgasbord of delights.

As soon as we were in situ we had plugged in the electricity. Leaving the water tank to slowly fill up we walked over to their terrace and here we saw the absolute beauty of the view that they have.

Casa Mae sits up high as though watching over the land which sweeps into the valley below. Looking down the steep garden, past their pool to a copse of trees nestling at the bottom, your eyes then naturally travel up and across rich green grass, olive groves and vines. Here and there, pretty villas dot about under shady tree's. To the right, spreading across a ridge is the town of Casalanguida. The lights were slowly coming on creating a little fairyland.

It's a stunning view.

We sat on the terrace with this vista before us as the shadows lengthened, sipping the cold Prosecco while catching up with each others news. We also grazed contentedly, as we chatted, upon the mouthwatering platters of food that Ann had laid out before us. There was a dish full of the Abruzzo delicacy...Porchetta which is slow cooked, melt in the mouth, falling off the bone pork. Plump green olives and slices of prosciutto. Gorgeous local cheeses with Ann's homemade quince jam. All of this served with the freshest of bread. It was a feast.

Meanwhile the dogs were delighted, they had their cousins to play with. It was their first time meeting Harvey. JD they already knew. Harvey and Betsy adored each other on sight, they immediately started playing, chasing each other here, there and everywhere until panting with exhaustion they settled down beside their two elders Archie and JD who were comfortably snoozing at our feet.

Abruzzo

Chapter 7

The next morning we woke to brilliant sunshine. Charlie and David were already outside on the terrace. I sat up in bed sipping coffee whilst Betsy and Harvey ran in and out of the caravan, jumping on and off the bed with great delight. I thoroughly enjoyed not having to be anywhere at any particular time before leisurely showering and joining the others for breakfast.

We were able to appreciate the house and its surroundings even more now in the full bright light of day.

We explored the land which includes an old ruin which was the original family home. The family who sold the property to David and Ann had later built the house that is now Casa Mae. A lot of this land slopes steeply down into the valley. They were in the process of terracing this to enable ease of planting. In the year they'd lived here they had done so much. Together they were creating a beautiful home that they loved.

Later that morning we all went up to the little town of Casalanguida and whilst there we saw Giuseppe a friend of theirs who invited us to his home. Giuseppe, who has now sadly passed away was a friendly lovely man. He had spent part of his life working in Canada so spoke some English. We sat around his kitchen table drinking cool soft drinks. Glancing around I noticed photographs on the wall of whom I assumed were his family.

Plucking up my courage, in Italian I ventured

"Is this your family Giuseppe?" or words to that effect. I'd lay bets on my grammar being completely wrong but, I had made that leap.

It is scary trying out a language in real life. I had been asking for things in shops and cafes , saying my Please's and Thank you's but here I was having to string together a sentence. To my delight he actually understood me and replied. David and Ann both looked at me with open mouths and said, when we got outside " Wow look at you speaking Italian" I had told David about the Italian language app months before, but when do brothers listen to their sisters!

However by that afternoon they had both signed up to it. So did Charlie.

The days flowed by in a relaxed fashion. We all gathered on the terrace for breakfast each morning then David and Charlie who had started a building project got stuck in to that.

David was glad of the help as he wanted to build a roof over the terrace and Charlie was pleased I'm sure, to be able to do something. My husband is not someone who finds sitting about for very long easy. He was in fact delighted to be going off with David to buy the materials and seeing his Italian day to day life including, of course the little local bar where to not stop for a cold beer would be downright rude.

Ann still had everyday jobs to carry on with guests or not, so I found myself with the opportunity to get my easel out and set up to paint the landscape.

We had all slipped into a rhythm. Stopping for lunch we would lay the table either on the terrace or at the spot they had carved out above the Ruin. It wasn't long before Charlie was talking about not only what a fabulous life David and Ann had here in Abruzzo, but also suggesting maybe we too should consider it. He and David had obviously been chatting away on top of the portico as well as over the cold beers in the local bar. It started to become a repetitive topic of his conversation and I laughed it off adding that as much I thought their place was nice and set in stunning countryside I absolutely could not see myself living up a mountain where I would feel cut off from everywhere and everyone, even more importantly a world away from Zoe and family.

As far as I was concerned that was the end of it.

We visited some of the surrounding towns and beauty spots delighting in the views and crisp clean air.

One morning we drove down to the beach with the dogs then had breakfast in the only cafe still open now that the season had ended. The croissants which here in Italy are called Cornetti were delicious. They come plain or filled with a variety of flavours. Making a choice...amongst them were apricot, pistachio, chocolate and cream was difficult.

Munching contentedly and sipping Cappuccinos under a warm sun that danced and glittered upon the bluest sea seemed absolute heaven in the middle of October.

One Saturday morning they took us to the market in Vasto. Vasto is a large town, a mixture as are nearly all Italian towns, of both modern life and the ancient past.

The old part of town stands proudly overlooking the Adriatic Sea. It's worth a visit just to walk along the wall walk as the views are simply stunning. On a clear day you can see right over to Termoli, with its harbour walls jutting out into the sea. The undulating coast line of white sand enhanced by the green of mediterranean plants.

Standing there with a breeze riffling through your hair it's not hard to believe the legend that says it was founded by the Greek hero Diomedes.

There are ruins of an ancient Roman theatre and baths as well as mosaics, marble columns and statues all proof of its history as a flourishing town under the Roman Empire.

The second hand markets are fantastic. Charlie and I are now veterans, especially of this particular Saturday market. I even have my favourite stalls. Some of the stall holders on seeing us call out in English 'Hallo's' and 'How are you's' but I'm jumping ahead of myself as this was still our very first visit.

The first thing that struck Charlie and me was the smell. No fusty musty scents here or the whiff of moth balls. The air was full of the scents of fresh clean laundry. Stalls of crisp white sheets in quality cotton. Hand embroidered table cloths and buttoned pillow cases. As this was October the winter clothes were out. Jackets and coats which on inspection ranged from high street labels to genuine Versace.

Having no charity shops here in Italy the second hand clothing is sold at these street markets. Italians in general are world renowned for their fashion and it seems to me that a lot of them discard seasonally to make room for the new thing on trend as many of the clothes are either unworn or worn only once. This is fabulous for those of us who like to bargain hunt.

On a very different subject as well as jumping ahead in time, I'd like to add for those of you who are gluten free, that in Vasto there is an amazing Gluten free supermarket which even has its own bakery. I didn't discover my own intolerance until a year ago in 2023 and was thrilled to recently discover this shop.

At first the days seemed to spread deliciously in front of us but then we became aware that if we wanted to do certain things we should start to arrange them. We all wanted to visit Pompeii none of us having done so before, and also the Amalfi Coast. I booked us two little caravans on a park close to the ruins of Pompeii itself.

I had also called Rosa Di Matteo who had invited all four of us over for lunch. It turned out that Rosa lived only about an hour and a half away in the neighbouring region of Molise.

San Martino in Pensilis. Molise

*C*hapter 8

It was a Sunday.

Sunday the 20th of October 2019 to be precise. Who would have guessed that this particular day was going to mark the beginning of a whole new chapter in our lives.

We had left all four dogs at the house. The sun was shining.

We were on an adventure. Molise was new to all four of us. We'd driven down the mountain with the sea in front of us (I always call it a mountain as it's a long way up... maybe it's really just a very high hill) At the bottom we took the right turn towards Vasto heading south to the border of Molise.

Right up until 1968 Molise and Abruzzo had been one large region but after the split Molise was little known, even to other Italians. There is even a joke about it:

'Molise non esiste' / 'Molise does not exist'

As you drive along the main road past Vasto you can see the town of Termoli in the far distance, it seems to curve out into the sea, below its walls are stunning white sands and shimmering blue water. As you get closer you are able to see the different coloured houses and cottages of the Old Town sitting within those old harbour walls.

We had no idea where our actual destination was. We did have the name of the town and Rosas address in the Sat Nav but beyond that we knew nothing about where we were going.

All the way along, from the moment we'd got to the bottom of David's Mountain, as we'd named it, we'd had the sea on our left and on our right green fields and olive groves interspersed with Vasto and the smaller towns of San Salvo Marina and Pettaciata. We now turned off and the sea lay behind us, we were driving along a valley road. To the left and right towns were hugging the hilltops. These hilltop towns all look so intriguing , with their ancient walls built to keep out invaders from so many centuries ago. The old stones bask in the sunshine with Olive groves and vines wending their way down the slopes. We then turned off to our left and drove over a little railway crossing. Looking up I pointed "Do you think that's where we're headed?".

Above us was indeed San Martino in Pensilis. From a distance it made me think of the Christmas carol "Oh, little town of Bethlehem" The truck climbed the hill as it wound round and round until suddenly we were there. We found Rosa's house easily and parked. She had heard the engine and come out to greet us. As is always the case with important people in your life the years just melt away. Charlie and I hugged her then we introduced her to David and Ann.

Mamma came out. Once again it was as if no years had passed at all and in we all went to Mamma's kitchen for the very first time.

This was to be the first of many meals in Mammas kitchen but at this point we had no idea of what to expect. Now I can hand on heart tell you that some of the best food I've ever eaten here in Italy has been cooked by her fair hand. All regions have their own specialities and unknown to us at that point , we were in for a real treat.

Rosas brother Gianni arrived along with his wife Rosella and their son Luigi, we hadn't met them before so, with more introductions, followed by the pop of a Prosecco cork we all settled round the table.

We soon had plates of steaming Pasta topped with a mouth watering ragu sauce. Conversation ceased as everyone's attention became centred on their food. It was delicious. The best ragu ever, and the Pasta was fantastic. Mamma had made the Pasta herself fresh for our visit as well as the sauce.

"Would you like some more?"

Of course all four of us foreigners held our plates out eager for more.

This was a huge mistake.

Yes, it was utterly amazing but if we'd known what was to follow we would all have politely declined. As the last of the sauce was mopped up and we attempted to discreetly adjust our waistbands conversation was resumed.

We were all now sipping on a very tasty wine.

The wine was made by Mamma.

We thought maybe there would be a little fruit or maybe a little dolce what we weren't prepared for was the large platters being laid out in front of us. On one was grilled sausage , oven roasted herb flavoured lamb chops and pieces of roast chicken and, I found out after I'd eaten some, rabbit.

Another plate was full of Molise's speciality dish Pampanella.

Pampanella actually originated right here in San Martino in Pensilis and is pork that is flavoured with sweet and /or hot ground peppers (in another book in the series I will tell you more) this was the only thing that Mamma hadn't prepared herself although I have no doubt that she can. There are special Pampanella shops here in town where you buy it by the kilo either cooked or ready to put in the oven and cook yourself. There is even an annual Pampanella Festival.

Plates of oven roasted potatoes were squeezed in along side bowls of brightly coloured grilled red peppers. Bowls of fresh green salad chopped and mixed, yes of course you guessed it by mamma herself glistening with their own olive oil.

She had reared the chickens and gathered their eggs, grown a lot of the produce as well as having produced the wine. It was all delectable and we were all full to bursting. You try to say, "No thank you" to an Italian Mamma who is urging you to "Mangia, Mangia" which means "Eat, Eat" especially when it tastes so good. On top of which you know how much effort had gone into this, well, there is no other term...this banquet.

Charlie , David , Ann and I all glanced at each other did we all feel as totally stuffed as each other?

A lesson was learnt.

Never ever accept a second helping of Pasta in Mammas kitchen.

Yes, you want those flavours back again.

Yes, you crave the comfort of that home made pasta, but,

DON'T DO IT.

Not unless you want to burst like a popped balloon.

All of this was followed by one of Rosas specialities, her scrumptious Tiramisu and then strong coffee.

The four of us Brits were intrigued to learn about the Olive groves and the harvesting as well as the vineyards and jumped at the chance to go and see them.

As we left the house the view stopped us in our tracks, somehow when we had arrived amidst all the hugs and introductions we hadn't fully appreciated it. Now we all stood and just gazed at the vista laid out in front of us. We had walked out of the house and across the garden with its fully mature shrubs and trees. Past a lemon tree in a large pot to a low wall with pots of basil adorning it. Here grass slopes down to an ancient terracotta dovecote which stands proudly against the blue of the sky. Chickens were contentedly pecking about below it, while beyond, the range of snow tipped Majella Mountains can be seen way over in Abruzzo. Between the mountains and where we stood, the town of Guglionesi stands high on the opposite hilltop to San Martino. In-between these two towns is the valley that we'd driven along earlier, which came from the sea and Termoli. Sure enough with barely a turn of the head there was the ocean.

A version of that view is now ours and I don't think that we will ever get blasé about it.

Even as I type I can glance up and see the snow on the mountain tops to the West, to the North is the sea.

Who would ever have dreamt of this on that afternoon, not the pair of us to be sure.

However, approximately ten minutes later when we'd said our goodbyes and profuse thanks to mamma we were following Gianni's car. Taking a left turn there was the sea spread out in front of us.

Right then, right there. On that road that leads down to the Adriatic Coast I turned to Charlie

"You know what, if you really wanted to live in Italy I would live here."

It was a throwaway remark, appreciation of the beauty of the area. An appreciation of the warmth and welcome we'd been given.

It was NOT a thunder clap moment of Wow this is where we should be. Neither were there any of my famous tingles and yet a little over a year later on 30 th October 2020 we would be moving here to this town lock, stock and barrel.

We stopped at the Olive Oil Co Operative first and watched from start to finish the different stages of production. Rosas' brother Gianni it turned out is the President of the SMIP Olive Co Operative, he is also the Mayor of the town. He is an unassuming man with a real passion for his town and birthplace. After studying then working in Milan he came back to Molise and invested in his local area building a factory which processes and packs fresh local fruit and vegetables as well as undertaking the role of Sindico / Mayor and the Presidency of the Olive Co Operative.

From there we followed Gianni's truck to the vineyards and an olive grove where we wandered underneath olive tree's and watched as the harvest was still underway. We tasted grapes straight off the vine, the delicious sweetness filling our mouths.

It had been a brilliant day. Seeing Rosa and Mamma again, renewing bonds of friendship, meeting Gianni, Rosella and Luigi. Not to mention stuffing ourselves with traditional Molise cooking and experiencing part of an olive harvest.

Now it was time to say our goodbyes and head back to the dogs.

Pompeii.

Chapter 9

We all bundled into the truck four humans and four dogs and set off towards Naples. The landscape noticeably changes as you go from Molise into Puglia which is further south and then south west to Campania. Our memories are of swathes of flat plains and vineyards as well as the hills that we'd become accustomed to everywhere in Italy. Around 3 and half hours from Caslanguida to Naples and our first sight of Vesuvius. Isn't it strange how something can be so much a part of your life in however remote a way. If you think on it, we learn about the Roman Empire from early school days. It is of course a huge part of Britains history, during the course of which we are taught the history of Pompeii and of the eruption of Vesuvius then one day there we are travelling along an autostrada watching it grow closer and closer. Of course I'm making it sound as though we were driving along in awed recollection of centuries past when in actual fact David and I were arguing in brotherly sisterly fashion, over whether or not this was the famous Volcano.

I was insistent it was, David adamant it wasn't.

In the end we made a bet... the loser was to buy cold beers as soon as we arrived. When we did arrive at the site we were all pleased and relieved especially the dogs who were longing to stretch their legs. The grounds were pretty, full of mature flowering plants and green verges where the Touring pitches were well spaced amidst them.

David and I went to the reception to check in, collect our keys and ask the all important question...I won the bet and grinned widely as the receptionist got 4 ice cold bottles of Peroni lagers from the fridge.

I wasn't however grinning after we saw the accommodation. Two dusty dirty looking static vans stood side by side. The pitch was shabby with a most unwelcoming set of grimy table and chairs. On opening the doors and inspecting the interior I didn't know whether to laugh or cry. However, Ann and I were soon laughing almost hysterically as it seemed we had simultaneously discovered the towels in the bathroom. With sheer incredulity I'd picked up this sorry looking piece of 'white' material from the towel rail to discover it had been cut, presumably in half and to add salt to the wound had a hole in it. Ann had found a similar piece of rag. We met in the middle, me hanging out of the window. We were holding up our towels in disgust and yet creasing up with laughter. When the hysteria had calmed and we'd sipped some of the cold beer we walked back to reception to ask if we could move, unfortunately it seemed that we had one dog too many to move into one of the chalets so it was here or try and find somewhere else. It was very hot and we were all tired so having scrubbed the table and chairs we sat and discussed the situation eventually deciding to stay put as finding somewhere that would take four dogs didn't seem an easy task.

The bedding at least was clean even though the top cover was stained. I pulled them back and examined the sheets intently to ensure nothing moved.

Our spirits lifted considerably on realising how close we were to the gates of the Ancient ruins of Pompeii. There was it seemed a glimmer of gold after all. (I always try to find the glimmer of gold or silver in any pile of poop that life unexpectedly throws my way)

It was just a short walk away and it was getting a little bit cooler. Being this much further south it was considerably warmer here than Abruzzo. Deciding this would be a good time of day for our visit we ambled along to the gates and having purchased our tickets stepped inside.

Now I think I've made it clear that I love history but it is important to say here that all four of us do. We were never going to do one of those kind of tourist sweeps, where a glance here or a glance there is enough…you know the type… enough to sit at a dinner party and say 'Oh yes darling, we did Pompeii last summer' No absolutely not, and one day perhaps I'll write about the time that Charlie and I were in the Toulouse Lautrec Museum in France.

But I digress because here we were standing on the actual streets of Pompeii and of the eight of us, four were over the moon. We didn't even get to see half of it, it's a huge area but what we did see we really saw. Some of the dwellings didn't allow dogs in so we took it in turns. One couple dog sat while the other explored. We were all enjoying just being there, walking on these very stones, gazing at paintings that had miraculously survived the centuries.

We wondered at this, whilst pointing at that. We walked until it started to grow dark then realised we had no clue as to where the exit was and could see no one to ask. Eventually we did find our way out and found a cluster of welcoming bar tables under a broad tree where we collapsed and drank Prosecco nibbling on nuts and crisps. We had all loved it and that made the whole experience even better. I would hate to go somewhere so special with anyone who had a blasé attitude to it. It doubles the pleasure when you get to share the experience.

A little further along the road we found a Pizzeria. The pizza's tasted amazing I had the Napoli speciality of fresh raw tomatoes, basil and mozzarella on a hot pizza base it was delicious. And, it was here that we came up with our lasting toast " Up Pompeii !"

If you are of a certain age you may remember or have heard of a comedian called Frankie Howerd and of the series 'Up Pompeii'. We are all four of us in that certain age bracket and even though we don't remember any details of the programme we do all remember the toga clad character and 'Up Pompeii'.

Positano

*C*hapter 10

Surprisingly we all slept well. Ann told me the next morning that she had removed their bed cover and had found an alternative in their case. I always have sarongs or wraps with me so Charlie and I had used some of those. As for the towel situation, we used tee shirts.

It was a short walk to the railway station. As we'd found a little bar and had our breakfast earlier we were soon on the train heading for our Amalfi adventure.

If you haven't taken a train in Italy before its worth knowing that after purchasing your ticket, and before alighting the train you need to get it clipped at one of the machines that you'll see around the station. The train we were on was clean even if not terribly comfortable, and the journey from Pompeii to Sorrento is only 40 minutes.

Arriving in Sorrento and not having already organised a trip we headed over to one of the Tour Kiosk's and booked a bus tour. The dogs were also welcome, they only asked that we sit at the back which we were happy to do. We only had a little while to look round Sorrento which was very colourful and full of cheerful bustle, certainly a place I'd like to visit properly one day.

The Amalfi Coast is just as narrow and twisty as you can imagine from all the films and photographs you may have seen and it is equally if not even more beautiful. I was glad for Charlies sake that he hadn't driven. For a start the truck was huge and secondly as calm and confident a driver as he is I would have hated to be a passenger simply because of the overhang of rocks and steep precipices coupled with nerve shattering bends that the locals seem to tear around in sports cars. Even the buses seemed to put on, to my mind anyway, an unnecessary burst of speed, causing a gasp here and there. I was also pleased for him because he was able to fully enjoy the stunning scenery.

Plus it didn't hurt that his hands were free and I was able to squeeze hold of them for reassurance at particular parts of the road. I am not saying any of this to put anyone off driving themselves, just to say that it is always an option to take either a bus or a boat tour so that you aren't the one gripping the steering wheel, as well as clenching your buttocks together for dear life.

Stepping off the bus at the first of the two scheduled stops we were all completely Wowed by the sheer beauty of what lay before us. Positano is absolutely gorgeous. To me it felt as if we had stepped into a technicolored postcard. The backdrop of sea and sky almost impossibly blue. The cliffs of high dark and craggy rock highlighting the tumble of pretty houses, villas and hotels in white or pastel shades. Here and there bright bursts of green and pink from flowering bougainvillea, pots of geraniums and lush ferns. Maritime pines and lemon trees. The lemon along with the olive is not only grown in abundance here but the famous tiles and potteries are painted with these iconic images. You will see the whitewashed shop fronts adorned with them.

We found a lovely looking restaurant for lunch. Fortunately being late October they had space for us. It was set on a series of tree lined terraces overhung with branches full of lemons. Our view was of the rest of the town tumbling away from us, down to the little bay where many small boats were pulled up onto the sand. We all ordered the calamari and when looking through my diaries for this book I found I had written 'best fresh grilled calamari ever'.

I've been fortunate enough to have meals in some lovely settings in my life and this is in the top 5.

I've mentioned the view as we looked down. Looking up was rather lovely too. Above the lemon trees that we sat beneath, the terraces of houses nestled in the craggy cliffs. Wherever you looked was beautiful. The scent of the lemons hung on the air and the cold bubbles of Prosecco were on our tongues. It was a lunch I shall always remember.

Being on a limited time we started to head back to the bus stop with all of us thinking we'd like to return. I for one would love to do it by a little boat stopping in the bays of different towns. Another time I hope.

I'll just add here that if you are booking a trip anywhere in Italy and wish to have lunch it is always best to do your research and book ahead. Lunch is taken very seriously here and if you want to have a good meal in a nice restaurant you will need to do this. Of course there should always be somewhere that you can buy a delicious slice of hot pizza which you will be able to enjoy whilst perched somewhere people watching or view gazing. It all depends both on what you desire and on your budget.

The second stop was Amalfi itself which didn't have quite the same effect on me. I don't think it's fair to judge it on such a short visit but to my mind it didn't have the same charm that Positano has. Perhaps on a future trip I shall get a chance to explore it in depth. My memory is of walking up from the quayside where all the buses had congregated. From there onto a wide street which was full of people with souvenir shops on either side of the road. There is a Cathedral on the right which is reached by a number of steps where it appear's to be calmly looking over all the action below.

Everywhere you look it is bright and colourful, the street slopes upwards, as Amalfi too is nestled under the cliffs. I am sure that once away from the main streets there are delightful parts to discover and to explore. If however you are on a time limit as we were, it may be worth reading up on and deciding whether you'd like a quieter more laid back vibe or the hustle and bustle of Amalfi. In hindsight I personally would have liked to spend the whole time in Positano and to have been able to walk right down to the little bay.

It had been a wonderful albeit exhausting day and we were all happy to get back on the train at Sorrento and head back to Pompeii. Unfortunately my feet and ankles had started to swell and by the time we got back looked more the size and shape of melons than my usually skinny ankles. (The only two parts of my body that don't fluctuate in size and shape...my ankles and wrists) Now they were also showing signs of oedema which was rather a concern. Having my legs elevated and keeping hydrated seemed the sensible course of action. The latter was easy enough but the former nigh on impossible in the uncomfortable room. I tried stuffing pillows, even the hole-y towels under my legs but with the mattress giving no support to speak of it didn't appear to be working.

I didn't want to make the decision to cut the trip short by a night and certainly wouldn't have done so if we'd been staying somewhere that was comfortable but I could see that walking around anywhere the next day would be stupid and I certainly wouldn't get proper rest in this accommodation, so I asked the others if they'd all mind if we headed back the next day, perhaps stopping at the volcano en route.

Vesuvius

*C*hapter 11

The next morning as we were packing our things Charlie and I heard a noise from outside.

It sounded like machinery but was so close we couldn't imagine what it could be. Pulling aside the strip of material that took the place of a curtain we were astounded to see two men digging up a patch of ground immediately outside David and Ann's door. I was dialling Ann's number when I heard Charlie exclaim "No surely not, it can't be!" I turned back to the window as Charlie finished " It bloody is, they're emptying the sewage!" By now Ann had answered , we were all on speaker phone. They too were looking out of their window in horror. Not one of us could quite believe it as we watched the sewage tanker back up to their front door. Needless to say it wasn't long before we were once again in hysterics. Well, you know what they say, if you don't laugh you'll cry. We did both. We were literally crying with laughter. Suffice to say we left the site with no regrets.

I name no names especially as this was over four years ago. Chances are they are now under new management or at least have had the static van's refurbished. There are a number of sites close to Pompeii. If I went again I would just check out the accommodation thats all I'm going to say. Or, don't travel with four dogs!

I would in all fairness like to add that first and foremost the staff were all very nice and as helpful as they could be. The location itself was perfect being in such close proximity to the Ruins of Ancient Pompeii as well as close to bars, restaurants and to the station. We all agreed that if we'd come down in our own vans (David and Ann have their own motorhome) we would have thoroughly enjoyed the site. Having our own creature comforts would have made a real difference and I wouldn't have felt the need to cut our trip short. But the accommodation that we were allotted was appalling. As I type I'm wondering why on earth I didn't formally make a complaint very likely because everyone was so nice. Again to be completely fair it is possible that it was the end of the busy season and renovations were about to start, although why on earth you would empty a sewage tank with guests less than a stones throw from it is anyones guess. Let alone stock a bathroom with bits of old rag.

Having left our hysterical laughter behind we went off to Vesuvius. As you drive up from the foot of the volcano you start to see glimpses of the City and The Bay of Naples below. The City is huge and sprawling but until you reach the parking area you can't imagine how big. At this time none of us had a desire to go into Naples itself. We were then, slightly put off by all the bad reports and stories you hear of it. In addition there were my very swollen ankles so there was no chance of me, at least ,walking around it. However now as I write this, I have visited Naples and stayed overnight there. I absolutely love it. It is an exciting vibrant City, totally different in character to Rome, Florence or Venice (I have yet to visit Milan, as of yet I've only driven through it) Naples is full of colourful characters and has such a wonderful atmosphere. The Neapolitans are an incredibly warm people, but all of this will be in the future and recounted in Book 2. For now we are on the slopes of Vesuvius arguably one of the most famous Volcanos in the world.

I am terrified of Volcanos. OK, maybe not terrified but I am very nervous about them...

I couldn't think of anything worse than standing on the craters edge and peering into the depths below, so for this reason alone I was now rather grateful for my melon like ankles and more than happy to wait in the truck with Archie. After waving off the others Archie and I had a short stroll so that he could enjoy some sniffs and do whatever he needed to before we settled ourselves comfortably in the truck. It had large windows with very comfy seat's and we were facing the bay itself. A real panoramic view. As I gazed around with my sketch book on my lap I noticed all the dead trees that dotted the slopes. Beyond this and out to sea are the islands. That day the weather seemed to be constantly changing, the sun coming in and out of clouds but whatever the weather the view itself was simply stunning.

They were gone quite a while. Archie slept while I read, sketched then snoozed it was very restful and I rather enjoyed it. By the time they came back though I really needed the loo and I was getting very hungry so when they did appear round the bend I was pleased to see them as well as interested to hear all about it. Did they see sparks or lava? No, no sparks or lava. That was a relief. I don't know where the fear originated from, maybe from junior school when we did a project on the subject. Perhaps it was when we'd studied the eruption that covered Pompeii itself I don't know but it really was a relief that there was no sign of movement especially as it was now lunchtime and even if Vesuvius wasn't rumbling my tummy was.

There was a Pizzeria a little further down the slope where we settled ourselves at a table with another amazing view. The pizza was of course delicious. We were after all in Naples.

Charlie, David and Ann had all enjoyed their walk around the crater. The three dogs obviously did too, as they were twitching and whimpering in their sleep at our feet alongside Archie.

Then we were on the drive home which was uneventful except that I saw my first Cinghiale. I was thrilled to see it and screamed with delight, Ann turned her head in time to spot it as well. It was standing by the side of a river and looked huge with enormous tusks.

At David and Ann's place there is a pack of about 30 of them including piglets which wander up from the copse below them, along their fence line. They can also regularly be seen walking up the far side of the valley. Charlie and I love seeing animals in the wild and had both been eager to see one, but as much as we'd scanned the area with and without binoculars neither of us had had even a glimpse. So yes I'd screamed out 'cinghiale' which is an incredibly difficult word to get to grips with (or, at least I found it to be).

It took me ages to get that word right.

If you're reading this and mouthing what the heck is a 'tusk bearing 'Cinghiale' and why wouldn't you be. It is a wild boar. A full grown male can be pretty huge and sport very menacing looking tusks.

Final week in Abruzzo

*C*hapter 12

As with all holidays there comes a point where the realisation sinks in that the days are no longer stretching lazily ahead but are rushing away instead. The first few days after Pompeii I needed to rest to allow the ankles to go down.

The weather was beautiful. Perfect for painting outdoors. I set up my easel with a couple of small canvases and oils, then using photos as reference that I'd taken in the Di Matteo olive grove I set out to paint a more personal Hostess gift than flowers or chocolates to take over to Rosa and family. We had all been invited for a second time and I wanted to take something with real meaning.

On the last Saturday Charlie and I drove over to Vasto where we had arranged to meet Rosa. We'd been here to the Saturday market but now were able to explore parts that we hadn't yet seen. There is the walk along side the old town walls with incredible views. It was a beautiful day so we could clearly see Termoli jutting out into the sea over in Molise. It's not difficult to imagine Ancient Roman townsfolk wandering along these very pathways clad in pristine white togas. Maybe, leaning on the warm stones to gaze down into the olive groves that cling to the hillside below. Perhaps, pausing at a trattoria for a dish of plump green olives with a glass of crisp white wine while others rush homewards for lunch. Vasto had been an important Roman town back in the day and as I mentioned in a previous chapter has reminders of those times within these old walls. Now it's a real mix of old and new. There are some lovely shops, lots of restaurants, cafes and bars. It's well worth a visit. After exploring Vasto itself either drive down, or walk (it takes approximately 30 minutes)to Vasto Marina. Down here there are sandy beaches and crystal clear waters. In the height of summer it's full of people at the lidos and restaurants. However even out of season you can find some restaurants open with their menu's of freshly caught seafood.

The following day all four of us had been invited back to San Martino for lunch. Unfortunately Ann was unwell so Charlie and I set off alone. This time Rosa took us for a stroll around San Martino where we stopped for a coffee at Bar Jolly where we were warmly welcomed. The pavement tables were full of people enjoying the sunshine. I surmised they'd all come out for a pre lunch catch up with friends and sure enough by 1.00 the street was starting to empty. We strolled around the medieval town walls drinking in...yes I'm going to say it again...the amazing views! Molise has, not just picture postcard views nearly everywhere you go, but stunning dramatic vistas better likened to large oil paintings, Masterpieces in a grand gallery rather than to a postcard. We both liked the town. Liked the feel of it...again tho' there were no fizz bang feelings of premonition. As we walked back down the hill to Rosas home the sea came back into view. I grew up in Hangleton which is a suburb of Brighton & Hove in Sussex. Hangleton itself is quite high and overlooks the sea from a distance. For me as for a lot of people who have grown up with, or lived by the sea it becomes an intangible part of you. Seeing it now at the end of the road felt so natural and I guess thinking about it now, like home.

We were warmly ushered back into Mammas kitchen and once again lunch was amazing. This time having learnt our lesson, we regretfully refused a second bowl of the homemade pasta and exquisite sauce ensuring there was plenty of space for everything that came next. We both felt so at home here. Rosa was having to translate back and forth but even so the conversation was flowing.

After this enormous and it goes without saying, delicious lunch we sadly said goodbye to Mamma not knowing when, if ever we would return to San Martino in Pensilis. After all who knew what the future would bring.

Charlie and I clambered into our truck and waved to Mamma until we were out of sight as we followed Rosa's car towards Termoli.

I now know this road so well and I never tire of it. The sea is in front of you all the way whilst to your left and right Olive groves and Vineyards along with fields of vegetables and grain. In the summer some of these fields are full of glowing yellow sunflowers thrusting their heads towards the sun. It's a fifteen minute drive from SMIP to Termoli through the little town of Portacannone and turning left just before Campomarino to join the dual carriageway. The sea is now on your right as fields and greenery give way to the outskirts of the town. You can see the harbour below as you cross the bridge that spans the lush gardens of the city park.

Following Rosa closely we turned off and came to a car park. Being a Sunday afternoon parking was free something we couldn't imagine happening in Brighton. It's worth knowing that when parking in Italy a Blue Bay means you need to buy a ticket from the machine and display it. If it's a white bay it's free to park. It's very inexpensive to park here in Molise especially when compared to the UK.

Termoli began as a small fishing port, much as Brighton started out as a small fishing village. Now, Termoli is a nice sized and busy town that happens to sit right on the turquoise waters of the Adriatic Sea making it a much loved tourist attraction. I immediately liked the central shopping area with it's wide pedestrianised thoroughfare. It has a large Piazza on the left where you can sit under the shade of broad trees or take a coffee at one of the cafes. The main street is lined with interesting little shops and boutiques. It was by now late afternoon and people had come out to stroll around, meet friends have an ice cream or early Aperitivo. It's from this modern shopping area that we crossed the road into the Centro Storico which is the old town nestled within its protective walls.

We started off to the right walking along the old cobbled streets and alleyways which reminded us of The Lanes in Brighton. Some of the little whitewashed cottages here belonged originally to fisherman and their families. It's very pretty with tubs of brightly coloured geraniums. Strings of deep red peppers tied from the balconies were drying in the sun. Here in the old part lots of little Seafood restaurants serve the fresh fish from that days catch.

We walked to the Cathedral. The first church, built on this site was in the 6th Century and that first church was originally built on the ruins of a Temple dedicated to Castor and Pollox, the twin half brothers from mythology. Going down to the crypt it is possible to see some of the ancient remains of the first church building. Returning to the main body of the Cathedral you can view the Relics of Saint Bassus of Lucera and of Saint Timothy both of whom are Patron Saints of Termoli. Saint Timothy was an early Christian Evangelist who travelled with Saint Paul and is mentioned in the New Testament.

Rosa led us along the alleys until we were back at the sea wall. We meandered along admiring cottages with trailing bougainvillea, the deep pink of the flowers complementing the hue of the sea especially as the sun was now sinking low. We came to a Bar where we were fortunate enough to find a vacant table with three stools right next to the wall itself. We were facing west with a cinematic view of an incredible sunset. Here we sat sipping our cold drinks as we watched the sun dip slowly behind the mountains over in Abruzzo the colours playing on the sea below and before us. This was definitely the life.

It was time to go. To say goodbye. It had been wonderful to renew and strengthen our bonds of friendship, we felt so comfortable together. Little did we know as we waved our farewells what was in store for us all.

The following day was the last of our Italian holiday. Happily Ann was feeling better and we made an impromptu decision to go to the Sangro River British Cemetery which the people of Abruzzo gave in thanks, for the British and Commonwealth lives lost in World War ll. We drove there along the Trabocchi Coast which, in my opinion is just as lovely as the Amalfi coast only without the terrifying bends and such sheer drops. It is so called for the fishing platforms that dot all along this part of the shore.

The Trabucchi which are literally fishing machines built upon wooden stilts date back from (at the very least) the 18th Century according to the earliest documents found in Gargano in Puglia. However some believe it's possible they actually arrived with the Phoenicians. Built in such a way that they are partially attached to the land, secured to the rocks on the shore but mainly jutting out into the sea itself which means that even in bad weather nets could still be cast even when it was too dangerous for the boats to venture out from this rocky coastline. These large nets were winched down into the sea needing at least four people to man them. Nowadays many of the descendants of families that once fished from them run them as very popular tourist attractions / restaurants. The menu is typically a set one of the daily catch. You will not only be eating the freshest of local fish and crustaceans possible but dining out on a piece of history that sits on, or rather in the sea itself.

The Sandro River British and Commonwealth Cemetery is slightly inland. It's a peaceful place, beautifully kept and of course infinitely sad as walking quietly around it is impossible not to feel for, and be touched by, all the young lives given for Peace in our time. I'm writing this at a time when the whole world seems to be teetering on the edges of yet another World War and I pray with all my heart and soul it doesn't happen. I recall thinking how tranquil it was. There were sheep grazing the other side of the stone wall that surrounds this Resting Place of so many. Listening to the gentle bleating and the sound of birdsong it's hard to imagine the horrors they all endured.

We spent some time quietly reading names, regiments and ages on the stones, perhaps even more poignant are those with no name inscribed. Whether known or unknown soldiers they all rest here on a green hill in Abruzzo surrounded by olive trees and the farmers working on their land. It reminded me that this is what they fought for-Peace and Tranquility.

The following day we said our goodbyes. It had been really special spending this time with my brother. I have touched briefly on the fact that our childhood had been traumatic and growing up I had always felt protective of him but life in general can get in the way of relationships and your priorities are then naturally with your own spouse / partner and families. Now in our middle years our weeks here in Abruzzo had brought us closer again which made saying goodbye hard.

Ann had made us all a delicious breakfast which we had on the terrace and were just debating over whether more coffee would be a good idea or not when we had a visitor. Giuseppe had come to wish us farewell and had so kindly brought us a bottle of his own Olive Oil, this was a big thing as the olive harvest hadn't been quite as good that year so we were especially touched by his kind generosity. Then it was time for the last hugs and goodbyes. With tears on my cheeks I waved and waved as Charlie pulled away and down the driveway. After all who knew when we'd be able to visit again. Little did we know that under a year from now we would be driving back up this very driveway to remain in quarantine because of a previously unheard of virus which had swept across the world claiming so many lives. That this new virus, in its own way helped us make a decision to make a permanent move to Italy.

The tears dried as we wound our way down 'Davids' mountain. I started thinking about Christmas and making our mincemeat even as we were travelling along the Adriatic coast road towards Rimini in brilliant warm sunshine. I was so looking forward to seeing the kids it seemed ages already that we hadn't seen them and usually we made our traditional mincemeat in October during the half term holidays. Of course we still had the journey ahead and were planning to stay in Aisne in France at an All year round campsite where we would be able to take Betsy and Archie to the Vet's to get their check ups.

By law this needs to be done inside a certain time frame for their Pet Passports to be stamped, so instead of staying near the harbour at Calais for a couple of days we had instead booked 3 nights there . Not only was there a Veterinary Surgery in the village but nearby was the World War 1 battle site known as Californie Hill. For now though we were heading towards Milan.

It was November the 5th and we were in tee shirts with the windows wide open really enjoying this route back. We stopped for lunch just outside Rimini glad of the huge sun shades that all the Motorway Services have over their picnic tables and drank in our last sight of the shimmering blue of the Adriatic Sea.

We were absolutely not prepared for the weather change that awaited us in Bologna and Milan. It felt as though we'd driven through some kind of weird Time slip as it suddenly felt so much colder. In moments we found ourselves driving into wispy mist before even worse, we were barely able to see the number plate of the car in front due to the thick icy fog that had descended. We took a wrong turning, bloody Sat Nav! It didn't help that it was getting dark not that we could see beyond the windscreen anyway. Eventually after what seemed ages we got out of Bologna passed through Modena and soon were on Milan's ring road. To our relief we found the Campsite, pulled up to the gates and I creakily got out and rang the bell. No response! I tried again and again. Pulling out my phone and retrieving the number that I'd called the day before to book our one night stay. There was nothing, no answer. OMG Are you kidding Me! I peered more closely through the gates and realised it was all shut up. The season was well and truly ended at this particular site. Had it been kids mucking around the day before accepting our booking? We'll never know the answer to the mystery but I was pissed off and now I had to break the news to Charlie who was tired and hungry and had just been manoeuvring an enormous and very long fifth wheel caravan in thick fog on unknown roads with the hinderance of a very annoying SatNav.

Next to the very closed gates was a restaurant, so attempting to reassure Charlie with a wave of my hand and a rictus grin I went cautiously in. They were so nice, very patient with the fact I couldn't speak more than 20 words in Italian but my smile was no longer stiff. It was now wide and warm, delighted by these people, especially when having listened to my tale of woe the lady said to me "Park outside. You can stay the night there" I didn't think I'd made myself clear, did she think we were in a car or maybe a motorhome. "Non preoccupare , please don't worry it's my land you can stay" Wow, I couldn't believe our luck I rushed outside glad to be the bearer of good news

" Charlie we can park up here and I've told them we'll be in to eat. It smells delicious"

So our last night in Italy was spent in a truck stop just next to Milan's ring road. Later when we'd eaten a very tasty meal in this lovely lady's restaurant, the fog and drizzle didn't seem to matter at all even as we trudged damply round the car park ensuring the dogs had their last wee of the evening.

Heading for Home

C hapter 13

Peering out of the window as we sat up in bed drinking our coffee the weather looked grey and felt distinctly chilly. No point in hanging around. We were soon on the road heading towards the Great St. Bernards Pass. It took a couple of hours to get there but when we did it was stunning. I am glad I wasn't the one behind the wheel however I thoroughly enjoyed being a passenger and admiring the views and shimmering snow covered vistas. We'd left Abruzzo the day before in what seemed to us Brit's summer weather, spent that night and this very morning in chilly fog and now, we were back to wearing our sunglasses against the sun reflecting on the pristine slopes. It all seemed rather surreal.

That night we stayed not far from the Pass itself at a place called Saillon in Switzerland. The snow covered Mountain tops surrounded us. It was so pretty. I could happily have stayed there for a couple of days but we needed to get on so the next morning we were on the road again straight after breakfast and a dog walk.

No offence meant to France, which is a lovely country but I find the sheer size of it's interior off putting perhaps because I'm a born and bred Brit, used to places being closer together. Even up in the Highlands of Scotland where the population is smaller it's not as far from one town or village to another so I feel a bit out of sorts when the road is long and empty and the surrounding countryside is vast. It wasn't my favourite part of the journey and I was very pleased when, with no problems at all we passed Reims and came upon the village of Aisne, finding the campsite easily and were able to park up, put the electric and gas on and open a bottle of Mammas wine. She had ensured we'd left with plenty.

Having arrived in darkness it wasn't until the following morning that we discovered we were next to a wide River. Betsy and Archie were very excited, not only at being able to be off leads again at long last but new and ever more scintillating scents were assailing their nostrils as we took a leisurely stroll. The owner of the campsite had kindly told us the local Veterinary Clinic times and general directions so we had made an appointment for the following afternoon. This is very important because without the official stamp from the Vet animals cannot enter Britain which is a good thing as Rabies was eradicated in the British Isles many years ago. Let's all keep it that way.

We headed off towards the village of Craonne. This whole area was the centre of fierce and seemingly never-ending fighting during World War 1. The German troops occupied the Chemin des Dames and had turned the Plateau de Californe into a fortress. Underground galleries including the Caverne du Dragon linked it to their other positions giving them the upper hand. The battle in this area known as the

Battle of the Chemin des Dames or as the Second Battle of Aisne was catastrophic for the French.

At the end of the war it was declared a Red Zone by the French Government who later purchased the land and had all remaining explosives completely cleared. It was then replanted with pine trees and turned it into a Site of Remembrance. There are two marked trails, one is about a 20 minute walk, the other around an hour. A 25M high Observatory Tower affords views for miles bringing home what a strategic spot it was. There are also two Memorials, as well as, a Memorial Garden which was designed by an Italian Artist for the fallen Italian soldiers in WW1.

As you enter the little Memorial Garden it at first seems to be no different to any other part of the woods however, you then begin to notice the Posts tipped with red. These mark the Fallen. The hollows are so formed to hold raindrops which symbolise tears shed for these brave men. It has been tenderly designed. Organic and thought provoking. Silence prevails. An absence even of birdsong under the pines as we walked along the trail where the trenches remain so clearly in places.

At the top of the tower Charlie and I placed pebbles on the Memorial Plaques one for our friend Stella's Great Uncle another for my Great Uncle Billy both of whom died in WW1. We stood in silence under the open sky accompanied now by the singing of birds and said our silent prayers for everyone who had fought.

The following day we drove to the Caverne du Dragon where we had booked our tour in English. On arrival we realised it was just going to be the two of us and within minutes Yves our tour guide had us both in tears. He simply said to us "Thank you so much". We, of course didn't understand but he then explained that his Grandfather had told him many times when he was growing up that the British had not once but twice saved their lives and he had told him that without them Yves would not have been born. I'd love to be able to recount more details but I didn't write more than that in my diary of the time. We were both enormously moved.

The tour itself is fascinating and I would highly recommend stopping in this area and visiting both the Caverne du Dragon and walking the trail on the plateaux. Originally a quarry dating back centuries the Germans had a spacious and dry headquarters. Some items remain, uncovered over time including day to day articles like food tins, a telephone as well as helmets and even someones boots. There are inscriptions too, carved onto the walls in German. It's a reminder that no matter what 'side' someone is on these were and, are, in all wars today young people who lived in a state of fear, writing letters back home to their anxious parents and loved ones. There is a Memorial of Light here in the Caverne another most poignant moment as you consider again all those lives lost.

Upstairs in the main visitor area are glass cabinets full of relics including an exhibition of brilliant models sculpted from spent bullets. Were these carved whilst waiting in fear to go back out into the fray?

Outside in the fresh air under the blue of the sky the feeling of sadness remained especially as our attention then turned to the giant black sculptures that commemorate the Fallen French Colonial Soldiers.Not all the recruits were only from Senegal but are so named the Senegalese Tirailleurs as the initial recruitment was in Senegal in West Africa. There are nine pieces standing tall and proud. Fittingly they stand near to the entrance as it was the brave Senegalese Tirailleurs who launched the attack on the Dragons' Lair on the 16th of April 1917.

It was a quiet drive back to the campsite as we gazed out on the peaceful scenery. Both of us thinking of all that we had seen and heard.

Back at the campsite we repacked the van for the journey to Calais. Our holiday had now come to its end. The dogs had had their check ups and their passports were stamped. We were looking forward to seeing the kids and to getting home.

The world turns upside down.

*C**hapter 14*

Home again and life returned to normal. We made our mincemeat together at Zoes house. This is our family tradition which started when Zoe was around 6 months old, (I have a photo of her in the pram holding onto the spoon over the big bowl of mixture). It goes like this...A day in October, usually during the school half term holiday. The kitchen table strewn with packets of raisins, sultanas and currents. Vegetarian suet, nuts and spices. Glace cherries glistening in a bowl, alongside which is a bottle of brandy. If I'm not shouted down I put on Slades 'Merry Xmas Everybody' CD with the volume at it's highest and we all set to. Everyone has a job, 'cutting up' the cherries with a blunt knife is usually the job for the youngest. When everything has been added to the large bowl it's time for the 'Stir up' to begin. This is taken very seriously. One at a time we take up the wooden spoon and stir the pungent (heavy on the brandy) mixture. If for example someone can't be there in person we phone them so that while another member of the family stirs for them, they can make their wish.

I love Christmas, in fact I'm called Mrs. Christmas by some friends, but the past two had quite frankly been awful. I had put my best and bravest face on because of the grandchildren but they had been such sad times. In November of 2017 my darling loyal Daisy had died. I have had dogs all my life and love them all, she was however very special. I still miss her. She was unexpectedly given 6 weeks to live and went in my arms.

And then LouLou died on Christmas Eve 2018. A loss that I still can't quite comprehend, not really. We had met in the Zappion Gardens in Athens, Greece over 37 years ago and just clicked. We belonged to the same Model Agency in Kolanaki and were introduced by a mutual friend. Lou was Krystal to my Joan…(it was the era of Dynasty). Like the character Krystal Carrington Louise was tall, blonde and beautiful. I was dark like Joan Collins who played the part of Alexis. Although we hadn't lived in the same country three quarters of the time that we had known each other we were just always a part of each others lives. She was Zoes Godmother and, my Best Woman when Charlie and I got married. I loved her family too. When her father George died she and her brother Simon did a reading at the funeral, afterwards she said to me "I didn't think I'd be able to get through that but then I caught your eye and you smiled at me and I did" That is what we did, what we'd always done we lifted each other up. I was devastated at not being able to fly out and be beside her when she was dying. And I was devastated for her Mum Jan, brother and two sons.

I remember that Christmas Day having troweled makeup on over swollen eyes and a puffy face trying so hard just to smile for the kids.

This Christmas Day of 2019 was very different. We celebrated altogether. Cyrus's Mum, Dad and extended family as well at a restaurant at the Marina in Brighton. It was a bright sunny day not a cloud in the sky as we took photos outside with the boats bobbing about on the water behind us. I glanced up from the keyboard as I typed those words, as one of the photos from that day is on our kitchen wall. It was such a wonderfully happy day and a bright cheerful Christmas memory after two ghastly ones. We had no idea it was going to be the last Christmas together for quite a while.

The New Year began as new years do, in our house anyway. I like to get all the Christmas decorations down at some point on New Year's Day, this is usually after Charlie has gone to bed. Even if I start out thinking oh, I'll leave it until tomorrow invariably down they start to come. I just love getting up on the 2nd of January to the fresh start even if that means everywhere needs dusting somehow it feels right. Of course I am simply gagging to put all the Dec's up again by the beginning of each November.

Charlies mum started to go downhill in January. Meanwhile on the News there were reports of a new Virus in China. As for most people when something is happening in your immediate family you tend to be focused on that rather than World events but the bulletins about this Coronavirus as it was being called, were starting to get more and more alarming and by the 30th January the first two cases were confirmed in the United Kingdom. On the 31st January it had arrived in Rome, Italy.

Mum died on the 29th February, a Leap year. She was 93 years old but that made the loss no less. No one is truly prepared for a loved one to die. Of course we all knew she had had a long and mainly happy life, that this day would come but when it does it is just so final. No time now to utter the words you wish you had said, no moment left for a warm embrace. Thankfully we knew that we had done the best that we could. We'd had some happy times at the nursing home altogether in this last year of her life and she died knowing how loved she was by all the family.

Throughout February cases in the UK were increasing but by the 29th February the total number of cases was 23. I don't want to write, only 23 because every case was a huge worry, however it did make you wonder if perhaps the news was scaring people unnecessarily. Sadly they weren't.

The news coming out of Italy was simply terrifying and on March the 8th the Italian government put 60 million people into Lockdown as Covid had now spread into every Region in Italy.

In the UK we were being told to distance ourselves and to wash our hands to the length of a verse of Happy Birthday.

Daily it seemed there were changes and by the 20th March we were told that schools would be closing.

On the 17th March I had started coughing so immediately self isolated. I'd been feeling a bit rough but with all the emotion of Mums death, the exhaustion of that last week of her life where we'd been with her as much as possible and on top of which my own general health I hadn't thought anything of it. On the Sunday it was Mother's Day. Zoe, Cyrus and Phoenix came to bring me flowers and we spoke through the window. Zoe and Pea made me laugh as Zoe was miming Keep back Keep back with a plastic rake and Pea was swathed in a scarf with Cyrus's gloves dangling from her hands. It was wonderful to see them even if only through the glass. We had no tests but the symptoms were covid like. Thank God it didn't get any worse but I did have to speak to my specialist nurse because my breathing became very laboured. And later to a doctor on the emergency number who told me to call an ambulance if the breathlessness worsened to the point that it occurred when doing literally nothing. Thankfully it didn't get to that point. Afterwards when I recovered I did too much too quickly and developed long Covid symptoms. We only realised long Covid was possible, never having heard of such a thing before, after reading an almost mirror list a Doctor suffering from it had written online.

Charlie too probably had it, he had muscle fatigue and chronic exhaustion. I'm saying probably because we don't know for certain that it was. However speaking to the specialist nurse and later to a doctor who both heard my breathing, they said it was likely.

Now in 2024 I know with positive tests I have had it twice since being here in Italy. Once in 2022 and then in September 2023 so I feel pretty sure we did have it back in 2020, especially with the long Covid symptoms which continued until mid July.

On the 23rd March the British Prime Minister Boris Johnson addressed the nation on live tv and told us all we had to stay at home, in our own homes and this would be in force from the 26th.

The UK was now in Lockdown. We would be able to go out only for essential items such as food and medicine. We were also allowed out to exercise but Open Air gyms were taped up and closed off as were Children's Parks. Libraries and even Places of Worship were closed.

Every day it seemed there was new even more awful news. Deaths had now risen to 422 in the UK. Now nobody was talking about scare mongering. By the end of March Italy's death toll was vast. It was terrifying.

WTF was this virus.

Due to the nature of his business Charlie was one of the fortunate ones, able to continue with work. The main part of his company was the installation of Sewage Treatment Plants. Cyrus too was able to keep working having a Plumbing Company. Those that could continue were not only able to continue earning a wage but also were not trapped inside for the majority of the day. Lockdown would soon start to affect all of us stuck in the house or flat.

We ourselves were very fortunate having a comfy home, plenty of space inside and out. We even had a Hot tub in our garden. I really felt for those that were short on space or access to outdoor areas.

On top of which we were walking distance from the beach or a two minute drive away. It must have been horrendous for families trying to keep children occupied as well as educated in the confines of a small flat or in one room.

'Clap for Carers' occurred for the first time on the 26th March becoming for many a highlight of the week, it was a chance to see other people, even if only from the other side of the street. Clapping and clanging of pots and pans became a way to let off steam.

News reports showed the Italians doing no such thing as, with the inherent style of their nation they completely Wowed us all. Cheering everyone up with Operatic outpourings across geranium adorned balconies. It gave everyone everywhere a sense of being in this together whether clapping , singing or bashing pots and pans.

Queen Elizabeth ll gave a television broadcast on the 5th April this was rare indeed. The Christmas Speech is of course part of the British calendar but now we were in a State of Emergency for the first time since WWll. Her Majesty spoke to us all as the matriarch of the nation. I found it comforting as like the Clap for Carers it was a unifying moment. The Royal Family were also in isolation indeed, the then Prince Charles had been infected with the virus himself.

I like everyone else missed my family. I wanted to hug them so desperately. Thank goodness for mobile phones we kept in touch with video calls and text messages and, as much as I missed the hugs the love was always there, the sound of their voices and laughter.

There was a ban on gatherings. We weren't able to attend Mums funeral which was in April. She had been planning it for years and every now and then she would phone me and explain something else she'd like done. Once many years earlier she had asked me to meet her in Burgess Hill. When I got there it turned out she wanted me to have a cup of tea with her in the Funeral Parlour apparently she went each week. This was where all her arrangements had been made...I was horrified to be taking tea there. Now, after all her careful planning, the Celebration of her life at her church and the gathering afterwards, none of it was to be. All that planning and it was nothing like she had wanted except, the last bit. She had called to tell Sue and me respectively that she didn't want any of us to go to the crematorium that she wanted us to see her off at the church. In that her wishes were sadly respected. We all said our farewells, sent thoughts and prayers from our own homes.

All these things - All that careful planning for something far off in the future that came to nothing.

The not being able to hold and cuddle our loved ones but still being able to laugh, share our thoughts and love over video calls and texts. The ever present fear that someone you loved would catch the virus knowing if it progressed to the lungs etc, you would not be allowed into the hospital with them must have been playing across my mind.

With all this going on, at some point the idea of buying the land in Italy was taking deeper root.

The land

Chapter 15

In early January Rosa had sent a video of a plot of land on the road from town towards the sea. It was 'that' road the one we'd been travelling along when I'd turned to Charlie and said so flippantly

" I could live here"

The video was taken on a very misty damp dull day but somehow we just kept thinking about it. Whilst it was on our minds in a light kind of way we had conversations about selling our place in Ferring and buying a flat in the UK. The thought then was to spend 6 months in each place. Somehow during this time of upheaval, stress and worry it all shifted.

Even as I sit here writing this I cannot pin point the one thing that caused a shift. All I do know is that Covid-19, the whole experience changed things.

We really never know what is around the corner. At one point in 2011 there I was laying in a bed in ICU hooked up to a Dialysis machine and lord knows what, having my life saved by the amazing staff at The Royal Sussex Hospital in Brighton. At another point I was only able to walk with the help of sticks and could barely function because of chronic crippling fatigue . I'd even almost sold my huge Studio easel thinking I'd never need it again.

And, my darling soul sister LouLou had died so young. With so many hopes and dreams in her heart.

Here we all were. Everyone in the world wondering what on earth lay around the corner. I do feel that this was somehow causing a shift subconsciously and very slowly. With all the doom and gloom everywhere the thought of the plot of land was a real gleam of light for us both. We began looking up on the internet for any information that we could find about Olive trees and how to care for them.

"Aren't we a bit old to be thinking about this?"

Then I found an organisation online called WOOFERS which is the World Organisation of Organic Farmers and Smallholdings. People travel around the world and help out with the harvest in return for food and lodging. That was interesting.

What about an income?

"We could do B and B couldn't we?"

" Yes, and we could do the landscape painting classes. The ideas we had all those years ago couldn't we?"

And so we thought and discussed. While Charlie was at work I was sketching ideas as to how the house could be designed to incorporate B and B guests. Rosa had sent us another video. This time it was a sunny day and we could see the sea.

I called her "Rosa, is that the sea in the video?"

"It is" she had replied "I'll video call you a bit later" Which she did and there it was blue and beckoning.

Then there was the problem of Brexit.

In 2016 the British public had been asked to vote whether they wanted to remain a part of the European Union or to leave and go it alone. Looking back now from 2024 it all seems to have been a huge mess. But it happened and however anyone voted or their thought process behind their choice makes no difference now. I actually wrote a huge chunk on how and why I voted but then I realised that by doing so it just opens up the chasm. There is no point in revisiting old wounds.

We can Learn from the Past but Living in the Past isn't a good thing.

Considerations of Brexit were a big part of buying land in Italy. IF we were going to do this and as you may have surmised the shift had happened somewhere and we were now thinking of lock stock and barrel living in Italy, we had to try and be there before the end of 2020 which meant we could retain all the rights of a European citizen.

After 2020 everything would change for anyone wanting to move into the EU.

Hugs Galore

Chapter 16

Oh my dear Lord is there anything as wonderful as hugging the ones you love.

We were all deprived of this simple but oh so important necessity of life. When we were able to and I got my arms around them I didn't ever want to let go. I remember those first hugs with Zoe and Phoenix (Cyrus was at work and Niaz at his Mums) I didn't want to let go of them, we were laughing, crying and just holding on to each other.

Life got back to 'normal' pretty fast after the initial reunions albeit there were still masks and hand sanitisers everywhere. In my opinion hand sanitiser is one good thing that came out of the whole awful time of Covid. I had always hated touching hand rails in a public place. I wonder if it's something to do with being a painter I seem to observe things that maybe others don't. For example the person picking their nose then pressing the bell to stop the bus. Another person coughing goodness knows what into their hand then grabbing the railing yuk. It turns my stomach so I'm all for the sanitiser.

People went back to work and to school. Slowly, very slowly life returned to how it had been. The kids were doing what all kids should be doing, going to school and hanging out with friends. Zoe and Cyrus were back at work doing what they should be doing. My friends were back at work and once again busy with their lives. Suddenly the daily texts and calls we'd all been making to each other during Lockdown grew less as we returned to the catchups that we'd all had before life became so small and confined.

I had never returned to the full energy force that I had once been before the AS and then Sepsis had changed everything. Once again it all started to feel very lonely. I had never told anyone what life really felt like for me after I got ill. I certainly never ever wanted to burden Zoe with how I felt or, my friends for that matter. Charlie was working all hours. I was very depressed. No one knew. Not even Charlie had ever known the extent of my dark thoughts and feelings.

Whenever I spoke to Zoe I would be bright and cheerful (I always tried to be the exact opposite of my own mother). I was the same with my friends, after all I told myself who wants to call or pop in to see someone who is constantly in 'woe is me' mode. It was scary to find myself facing that lonelier life again. Physically, during lockdown, I had been alone while Charlie was at work but everyone was 'in' the Covid situation of being stuck at home which in turn meant we all had more time for each other, for calls and texts.

Thoughts of Italy and thoughts of living on our own piece of land, of Charlie and me working together and creating not only our permanent home but a place for the children to come to whenever they wanted to, an inheritance for them in sunnier climes. These daydreams were the highlight of my once again lonely days. I was now coming round to the idea of full time living in Italy.

So, we put our house on the market in June.

All flights had been stopped or restricted for obvious reasons so like anyone wanting to travel abroad we were waiting for the flight paths to open up the world again. August 2nd was the first date available to us. Our tickets from London, Heathrow to Bari, Puglia were booked. Our friends Karen and Rob with their dog Ruby were coming to stay and dog sit. To say we were excited was an understatement.

We had now fully accepted that this was no longer a holiday home idea but a full on move.

Everything that had happened seemed to inch by inch move us along to that conclusion. Of course the first person we spoke to about it was Zoe. She was our priority.

If Zoe had said at any point 'No I don't want you to' then quite frankly I wouldn't be sitting here writing this book. Surprised she may have been that we had decided to emigrate but she was also very supportive and happy for us. I think she could see that we needed something more than we'd been getting from life.

August 2020

*C*hapter 17

At Bari airport we were hit by that special blast of heat that you only experience when arriving at warmer countries. It's a waft that brings excitement and pure uplifting pleasure. Coupled with the fact that we'd been in lockdown and now allowed out into the big wide world once again made us feel as gleeful as you can possibly imagine. If I could have skipped down the steps and onto the tarmac I would have, in fact I may even have done a cartwheel.

Bari is a two and a half hour drive from San Martino in Pensilis and is a pleasant journey along the Autostrada with beautiful scenery. Along with fields of produce, Olive trees and Vineyards you'll be able to see some of the Trulli Houses dotted about. These are particular to the region of Puglia in Southern Italy. A Trullo is a traditional dry stone hut with a corbelled roof. In the past they were often built as temporary shelters, storehouses or even as permanent dwellings. The actual technique dates back to prehistoric times using limestone, stones and boulders. Whitewashed, with their characteristic coned roofs they are a special feature of Puglia's landscape. Nowadays they are popular as Bed and Breakfast and holiday destinations. One place well worth a visit to see them is Alberobello which is a Comune of Bari. This village full of Trulli houses has been a designated UNESCO World Heritage Site since 1996.

However we didn't see Alberobello as we were heading northwards towards Molise. Rather than the ease of the Autostrada we had on this first journey out of Bari taken a wrong turn and followed a smaller road. As I mentioned way back in this story I'm not a great fan of the actual journey wanting instead to get to my destination. However this was post lockdown. This was post 'Upside down World'.

It was a wonderful feeling to be out. Out of the house out of the everyday. Wonderful to be back in Italy. It was very hot so when I saw what I thought was a fruit cart up ahead my mind went straight to Kent cherries being sold by the side of Sussex roads and country lanes and my mouth began to water but before I could say Stop I saw the table was empty. Turning to Charlie

"If we see another one lets stop and get some fruit"

However the next person we saw didn't have a table....Had they sold the baskets along with all the fruit?

Then it dawned on us. A little further along a woman in a bikini stood on the side of the road in sexy stance holding only a bottle of water. Ah, Ok. The penny finally dropped. Grazie Dio we hadn't stopped and asked for a bag of oranges or even worse a couple of large melons. Mortified at ourselves and our stupidity at assuming we were going to buy fresh fruit and thinking of all the myriad connotations of how that conversation could have gone we shook our heads and carried on. It wasn't many minutes though before I was worrying about the poor girls and women. I only saw one with a sunshade. Did they have sunblock or enough water? It was still blazing hot.

Charlie broke into my train of thought and asked me to check the upcoming roadsigns. Hoping there would be a name I would recognise I was delighted to see a sign for Termoli and also for Campomarino where we were to turn off. We'd booked a Bed and Breakfast just outside a place called Nuova Cliternia which is five minutes down the road from San Martino in Pensilis. It was a charming place and the room was comfortable.

We were here at last and longing to see the land. First though we were due at Rosas for lunch so after a quick shower and change of clothes we drove up the road into SMIP. It was so good to see them all, the whole family were there. Although we didn't hug maintaining a physical distance it was just so good to all be together. After lunch we got into the car and followed Rosa down the road. Down 'the' road , the one with the sea at the bottom. We drove past the Olive Co operative on our right, past the Builders Merchants again on our right then we saw that Rosa was indicating. We went past a sign warning cars to slow down for Deer before she slowly pulled in to park on a kerbside.

Here it was. NOW I had my tingles.

I remember looking up at the tree's. The beautiful olive tree's and just feeling it was so right. Making my way up the slope I was desperate to see the sea view, I could see peeks through tangles of brambles then glimpses through the giant bamboo stalks. At the bottom I knew I'd have a proper view from seeing Rosas videos and yes there it was.

In my mind I was Sold.

Charlie thinking in more practical terms was inspecting the well. I was excitely rushing about with Mamma as she was showing me the Mountain view.

"Oh wow Charlie we can see the mountains from here too"

I'd already found a spot that I could see in my imagination as a wonderful place to lay on a sun bed as the sun got a little lower in the sky.

There was however also another piece of land to look at, Rosa had told us about it and had sent photos. They were intriguing, you could see the sea. It also seemed wider. When restrictions in Italy had eased and people could once again travel from Region to Region we had asked David and Ann if they would drive over, take a look and video call us. They had gone to what I can only call 'our land' first . They parked where, in a couple of months time we ourselves would be parking then walked up the gentle slope to the brow of the hill whilst the whole time on a Video call to us. We were watching eagerly and I was interjecting with

"To the right, to the right what's that?"

While Charlie was asking about the well.

"Is there water?"

David and Mamma threw stones down and we could hear the satisfying plop as it broke the surface of the water. Meanwhile Ann and Rosa were approaching the back entrance, which at this time was a wide gap between trees and brambles. When David and Mamma had caught up they all walked up the lane which believe it or not had once apparently been a main road into SMIP it was very similar to a country lane in Sussex until, that was, they moved the camera and the view swept across Olive groves and down to the sea. "Thats the Tremiti Islands out there" Rosa was saying, but we couldn't make them out on the phone screen. When they had arrived at the other piece of land that was for sale David stood back and showed us as best he could from the opposite side of the road while the others walked around. I was a bit put off by a large grey wall which turned out to be a Mechanics workshop and also was a bit put off by the fact that a funeral director lived just behind. Whilst I'm sure he didn't bring his work home with him the thought of seeing a Hearse drive past daily, especially after the Pandemic and continuing death toll around the world didn't endear me to the place. Anyway to be fair my heart was already lost to 'our land' but it would be silly not to look at others especially as we hadn't even physically seen it as yet. David felt that he liked the second more but Ann preferred ours. We would have to wait and see for ourselves but we weren't going to poo poo it until we had. Well, not entirely.

Now we ourselves were standing on the plot and here was Charlie gazing into the well and dropping stones down it to satisfy himself with the plop plopping sounds. When he had had enough we all four of us turned to the back entrance just as Ann and David had a couple of months previously and walked down the little grass covered walkway past the entrance to a smaller grove of olives and out onto the back lane. We were retracing their steps as when they had done the recce for us a few weeks previously.

It was a lovely afternoon. The lane was reminiscent of many back in the south of England with the sun dappling through the leaves. We could hear a donkey braying nearby and a couple of dogs laying in their gateway lazily lifted their heads gazing sleepily at us.

This second piece of land had a wide frontage and was level, something 'our' land was not. To the right was the large concrete building that we'd seen on the video call, although all was peaceful right now you had to wonder what kind of noise would come from there. Directly opposite were cattle and geese. Whilst Charlie and I love animals I'm not sure we'd be loving the sound of geese first thing in the morning although I wasn't really sure if geese were noisy. Behind the land was the Funeral directors house with a driveway that went alongside the border. There would be no avoiding the hearse as it went back and forth. To the left though were horses and a friendly dog and we could see the sea.

But there were no Tingles.

Heading back down the lane again Charlie was saying that he thought maybe this second plot had been better as it was level ground but even taking the lack of Tingles out of the equation I didn't like the idea of the concrete wall let alone car engines being revved and goodness knows what else. I was more interested in the Lane, in the fact that it led into our lands back entrance, and enjoying the way it curved downhill slightly and how the sea came back into sight. It really was stunning. And, very like Sussex.

Rosa had arranged for us to meet a friend of hers to view another plot. This one was on a little road that turned off to the right from the back lane. Leo met and showed us around. More olive trees and a stunning view of the islands. This lay sheltered in a valley and was away from the road into SMIP. It was lovely and had donkeys and goats beautifully housed and well cared for next door. The price was also much lower, however, as lovely as it undoubtedly was there were two important things missing. Firstly if we wanted to have Bed and Breakfast guests as well as Painting Courses in a studio/gallery on site then it was much better to be more easily accessible. Secondly and perhaps more importantly, there were no Tingles. I realise I've mentioned them a lot but they were very important.

I knew my heart was up the road. Not down here in this pretty valley.

Over the next few days we would look at a couple more plots always going back to 'ours'. Charlie couldn't get his head around moving the olive trees. This would be needed to make way to build a house. Would they, indeed could they survive a move?

When Rosa realised Charlie's dilemma she abruptly told us to get in her truck (my Italian sister can be quite bossy sometimes) and off we went. Having no idea where we were going or why we just gazed out of the window at the fields of sunflowers. I'd had no idea sunflowers grew like that here. What a fabulous place to bring a group of painters. The landscape alone was a painters dream, add fields of brightly swaying sunflowers and this was ideal for those Art Holidays that we had dreamt about all those years ago.

Rosa pulled up at a large white property

"This is my cousins place" she said by way of explanation. Wide trunked ancient looking olive trees stood in a beautifully landscaped garden leading to a swimming pool. In the near distance the sea. This place would be ideal for a film location it was so beautiful. The reason Rosa had brought us here soon became clear as we walked up to inspect the olive trees. We were delighted with them and wondering exactly how old they were when Rosa explained that while yes they were very old they were only recently planted in this spot. Her point had been to show Charlie that yes, the trees could be successfully moved. That was the moment when Charlie had his tingles.

Or, if not tingles then his moment of 'we can do that'.

It was a brilliant way to set his mind at rest. Yes, Rosa can sometimes be a teeny bit bossy, but it's in a wonderful way and I do like to tease her for it.

Are we really going to do this?

*C**hapter 18*

That night back at the B & B we lay on the bed listening to the incessant chatter of cicadas through the open windows. A light breeze played across our skin as it wafted through the mosquito nets. Dogs barked in the distance, an owl softly hooted. These were going to be the sounds we would be hearing from Casa Phoenix.

By now 'our' land had a name. This was always going to be the name of our house whichever piece of land was supposed to be for us. Now that all Charlies reservations had dissipated he was as fully on board with 'our' piece of land and, as besotted as I was.

Let the excitement begin.

I'd known that I shouldn't try to persuade him. It was important that he came to his own decision and now that he'd resolved the tree problem in his own mind he was full on, all systems go. I can't say our excitement wasn't tinged with fear because it absolutely was. In fact all along the way fears and doubts were going to rear their heads and gnaw at us. Being on the same page indeed on the same paragraph made everything easier. At no time was one dragging the other into this. On the contrary we were grabbing hold of each others hands and leaping forward into the unknown.

After we'd visited Rosa's cousins she had taken us back to Casa Phoenix where we wandered slowly around hand in hand leaving Rosa on her phone talking to the owners.

They had been adamant that they wouldn't accept any offer below the asking price of 35,000 euros and we weren't about to quibble. The plot down the lane was less money but this already felt to us as though it was 'our place'.

We made a video that we sent to Zoe but as I finished I glanced up to see Rosa was shaking her head saying

" I don't think the owner will be able to come to Molise, not before you leave"

Our hearts plummeted, any teeny remnant of doubts about making the offer that may have lingered were swept away when faced with the prospect of it not becoming ours.

"Don't worry" said Rosa "Leave it with me". Easily said but not so easy to take heed.

However as I have often, fondly told Rosa she can be like a dog with a bone and thank God for it. Back in her kitchen with cups of tea in front of us Rosa was talking animatedly with Mamma before dialling another number where upon a new stream of Italian was pouring forth not one word of which I could pick out. With the phone placed back on the table she looked up "Problem solved" she said with a wide smile "We can go and see the owners cousin tomorrow afternoon".

I'm not sure how much sleep we actually got that night knowing that the following day we would be speaking to the owners representative and would know then if our land was actually truly going to become ours. Excitement and nerves must have played a part in us finding it difficult to drop off to sleep.

One thing I do remember is turning to Charlie and asking "Are we really going to do this?". To be honest I think this was an ongoing question. It was really bloody scary but also so exciting.

We woke the following morning feeling energised, doubt free and very excited. It helped that Zoe had replied to our video, had loved it and was excited for us. So after a breakfast of delicious pastries freshly baked by our hostess we were ready for Rosa when she collected us.

Our meeting wasn't until 5pm in the afternoon so the day was ours.We were off to the beach in full holiday mode.

Summer in Italy, at least along the coast is all about the sea. Going to the beach is a way of life, a culture all of its own. I grew up in a seaside town and each summer we spent every day possible on Brunswick beach in Hove. It is however an entirely different thing here in Italy.

In the UK we would pack sandwiches and bottles of diluted squash, towels and swimsuits all the usual paraphernalia however we would also make sure we took thick jumpers. The weather could and often would change in an instant but we'd only leave the beach if it rained hard, so the boot of the car would be crammed as often the Lilo's were still full of air. My mother was one of a kind not only was she divorced. This was during the 1960's and at school I remember being one of only a very few who had divorced parents, but she also had a driving license. For a woman to drive a car and it to be seen as something unusual might seem incredible to any one of 45 years and under to contemplate however it was quite rare and especially where we lived on a council estate.

She would bundle us into the car and off the estate where we would spend the entire day swimming and playing with other kids whose parents were sun worshippers. We were bronzed and bare foot. Brighton & Hove beaches are pebbly so our feet were like leather and we thought nothing of running up and down from our towels to splash in the English Channel.

Going to the beach in Italy means either hiring an umbrella at one of the many Lidos all along the promenades or, taking your own and setting up on a public stretch of beach usually in-between the Lidos (this is a handy thing to do, as when you need refreshments or the loo you can visit the cafe or restaurant at the closest Lido to you). Another option is to take a drive out of the main town and find beaches with next to no one on them, again taking your own umbrella and sun bed.

To Charlie and me the beach in Termoli where Rosa rents her umbrella was like a different world. Certainly a far cry from the beaches of my childhood. Each Lido has a restaurant with shaded tables overlooking the sea. Life guards sit up on their perch ensuring your safety. There are bathrooms of course and most have lockers and outdoor showers. Some have play areas for younger children and, or a table football game for all. Between the restaurant and the sea the Lido's area is covered with umbrellas. Each Lido having it's own colour. Very handy for when you return from a swim or a walk along the sand. You can rent the umbrella for the day, even half a day, a week or for a month. Most Italians rent their umbrella for the whole season and stick with the same Lido for years. This way they work their way down to the Umbrella in the coveted front row where there is nothing but a short stretch of raked clean sand between the tips of your toes and the clear topaz water as it gently murmur's inwards and out.

Rosa has a front row umbrella which is where we found ourselves. We lay listening to the wash of the tiny waves, wondering if the whole Covid thing had actually just been a bad dream, or rather a terrible nightmare. It didn't seem possible that it was still happening, people were sick and dying in the hospitals. The people with very weak immune systems still isolating and yet here we were enjoying the warm sun on our skin surrounded by others doing the same. It was so good to hear the laughter of children playing in the sea and to see people walking up and down in the shallows chatting away.

Inside restaurants, bars and shops as well as on public transport it was the law to wear masks. We had worn the obligatory face masks on the flight over as well but here laying on the beach and when swimming in the sea it was as if nothing had happened. I lay on my back in the clear waters of the Adriatic letting it gently lull my mind along with my body. We had been fortunate not to have lost close family or friends to this ghastly virus but it had taken its toll on everyone and it was just so amazing to let go of all the tension and let the sea take the weight of it all from me.

Under the shade at the Lidos restaurant eating fresh calamari fried in a light batter with a drizzle of lemon and a large salad . We sat with our sun kissed skin still tingling with the salt from our swim, looking over at the simply beautiful sight of Termoli's old town standing as it does within a high protective wall. It's castle, church towers and prettily painted houses. Was it really possible that we would actually relocate to this amazing place?

If we were we had to think about getting back to the B & B having a shower and looking presentable before our meeting with the owners cousin back up in San Martino.

The owners cousin who was expecting us opened her door along with her daughter. They invited us to sit at the table. We all sat. Rosa introduced us and we managed to say Buon Giorno after which we wisely left all the talking to Rosa although we tried to follow the gist of it we couldn't understand a single word. Maybe we wouldn't have been able to anyway however it was impossible because they were speaking in the local dialect. All Italian towns have their own dialects which even today throws me out completely and renders all that I have learnt useless so its easy to picture the blank looks on our faces as we at least tried to look vaguely intelligent and interested in what was going on. After listening to Rosa the owners cousin called the owner. Another unintelligible conversation ensued, at one point it sounded as though a huge argument was taking place but when I tapped Rosas leg and raised an eyebrow at her she just smiled reassuringly. I could see I was going to have to try and master the art of patience if we were going to live here as nothing seemed to be simple and straight forward.

I was itching to get out my phone anything other than sit there feeling gormless but all of a sudden the lady of the house was standing and offering us coffee. Her daughter was smiling and Rosa proceeded to explain that the owner would accept our offer of the full asking price, but, we would need to give the 5,000 euro deposit on trust.

Usually this would be done officially with a Notary however with no time to do so we would draw up a Private Agreement recognising that the deposit had been paid. I would not recommend this as a general practise however in our case we knew the family could be trusted because they were friends of Rosas' family. In a small rural town such as SMIP this means a lot. Of course it would still be in writing which although would mean nothing in a court of law was a record of sorts. As we had and still do have, complete faith in Rosa and all her family, coupled with the fact that we had a flight back to the UK in 48 hours we were more than happy to do it this way. The alternative was to possibly lose the land.

We also had to get our Codice Fiscale which is the Tax Code that you need for just about everything here in Italy. We certainly needed it in order to open an Italian bank account and transfer funds to pay the deposit.

The next morning there was a light summer shower as we joined a queue of masked people outside the Ufficio delle Entrada. All this happened in a whirl and as much as I know it happened it seems surreal that it was so fast. Rosa was simply amazing and helped us through all of it. We were so fortunate having her help, I can only imagine the nightmare of trying to sort things out without a native speaker beside you.

With our bank account opened and a transfer being made we were ready to see the owners cousin once again. This time with a private agreement typed out ready for signatures. Our money wouldn't be transferred in time for this afternoon's meeting so both parties were on trust. I've always been of the belief that when things are meant to be, you nudge the door (or opportunity) and it will open up. It appeared that this was meant to be, a feeling that was confirmed for us again and again in future months.

In a blink of an eye we were back on the plane. We went from a week of more or less 'normal' life back to face masks, social distancing and a sense of ever present anxiety. We hadn't looked at a newspaper, or watched the news. On our phones we'd caught snippets but had been far too occupied to pay much attention. In short the week had given us a complete respite from the immersion of covid-19. In Italy people wore their masks, used hand sanitiser, adhered to social distancing and fist bumped but overall there was an air of normalcy. Perhaps because it was August, the sun hot and soporific. After all the fear and those dire months at the beginning of the year Italians were relaxing into their summer routine.

Emotional Rollercoaster

*C*hapter 19

We were back and hit the ground running. The house had now been on the market for a couple of months. It felt frustrating not having more viewings than we'd had but people were cautious and each appointment had to be Covid aware. Meanwhile we had to start sorting out what to keep and what to not. Daunting task when you climb up into the attic space and count the number of boxes that haven't even been opened since the last move seven years previously. One thing was certain every card, note and letter that Zoe had ever given us was in the 'to take' pile.

Books. There was no way I was letting go of books. There are certain books that I read again and again. A few years will go by then its like catching up with an old friend. Also I have wonderful surprises when I revisit them, an inscription from Zoe. A note from LouLou, of which

I came across several, each time a jolt but a nice jolt. Reading them as with her letters I can hear her voice. Charlie was the same about his LP's and CD's. We both had several boxes in the 'Italy' pile already. Piles of canvases too, and as for Christmas decorations don't get me started. There was no way we were going without them. Then there were Phoenix's toys and her lovely wooden rocking chair we'd bought in Bath and manoeuvred through the crowds of the Christmas Market balanced on top of Daisy's doggy ride on. All of these memories make up the patchwork of our lives. Every now and then Charlie would come out with things along the line of "What do you want that for?" Or "Oh my God really, why?" This especially when I was frantically looking for the lid to a large tub of Duplo "Because if Zoe and Cyrus have another baby we'll want this" and, I thought to myself 'this' while grabbing the Hamley's dolls house I'd bought for Peanuts second birthday.

Now that we eventually have a house again and most things have been unpacked I only have to glance up and look around to have all those memories enfold me. I don't feel any further away emotionally from Zoe and family than I did in Ferring because they are always with me.

Plus Zoe did get pregnant! Now when Gigi comes she'll have the Duplo to play with.

Furniture and storage what to take and what to not, we had to start thinking of those things. I had some numbers to call. There was a man with a van who did trips to and fro. He didn't get back to me. A couple of companies who asked questions and gave vague quotes. Then I found the company with the right sort of quote but had to leave every thing up in the air when it came to dates because 'How on earth did I know!'

It was all very discombobulating but at least the money transfer had happened and the deposit was sent and received. We then transferred the money for the balance of the land to our Italian account. We were truly blessed with an Inheritance from Charlies mum, Doreen. It was this money that we were buying the land with. Everything else would be from the sale of our house. Again it was a sobering thought that we were uprooting our security and heading off into the unknown.

We now had an interested party for our house but they hadn't yet had a firm offer on theirs. It was all a rollercoaster. Meanwhile as it was August most business's in Italy are closed for most of the month which meant not being able to make an appointment for the Notary.

Added to the carousel of emotions was the constant self examination. Top of this list of course was about leaving the kids. I had many sleepless nights over it however the bottom line was this. Their lives were full. Zoe and Cyrus had, and still do have successful businesses. Phoenix and Niaz were getting to the age where their sleepovers at friends etc were priority. This is all as it should be. Just as I never intended being the granny in the corner that was no fun, neither did I want to be the Mum and Grandmother who was pleading for the family to spend time with us and being a pain in the backside. When we are all together we have the best times and I'd rather take that then have grandchildren being made to visit once a week when they'd rather be with their friends. We are truly blessed to have the relationship that we all have and whilst I knew this and still know it, I couldn't help the feelings of guilt.

Every time it crossed my mind to call a halt to the madness I thought back to the past few years, to the loneliness and depression and the over riding thought was this "I do not want to grow old in a box, I want to live, to REALLY live. I don't want this to be it. A slow descent to older then to old age".

Also this purchase wasn't only for us it was and is for all of us. As I write this we are preparing for their first visit, they are due in May. We've been back to the UK to see them of course but until the house was built and ready for a toddler they've been unable to come to us. You can imagine my excitement. Yes! I did say a toddler GiGi will be three this July!

She arrives a little further along in the story. For now it was guilt enough leaving two grandchildren let alone three.

My solution to some of the guilt was to book myself an appointment with a tattoo artist in Worthing. I decided on the design and booked it in, nervously! I felt I should be stamped somehow as strange as that may sound. I already had a tattoo from way back in the mists of time when I'd had a Swallow inked on my shoulder and had had neither the inclination or reason to have another until now. Now I wanted the girls names on my arm.

Whilst I was wrestling with the emotional, Charlie was sorting out our 5th Wheel Caravan. Our month or more away in the LouLou Bella had made us realise that living in it full time would very probably prove difficult. For a start it had only one slide out and no proper wardrobe / storage space at least not enough for year. Whilst the weather in Molise is milder most of the time (we'd been doing our homework) it can get very cold around the end of January into March. When the rainy season comes it's heavy and the wind can whip up. Equally a mild balmy spring can become a ferocious ball of fire in August. Storage was important. Charlie found a company who were interested in a part exchange and who, despite covid restrictions were able to come down to Worthing. Having seen both photos and videos that Charlie had sent they brought down the quad slide which we looked over as they looked over ours. Both parties being happy we paid the difference and away they drove with LouLou Bella. We cried. Silly of us, maybe , however looking back I think it was because this was the first in a series of farewells and the biggest and most important was looming. Again I reminded myself we weren't just moving abroad to another four walls, exchanging one life for another just with distance between us and our loved ones. We were going to create and built a new more fulfilled life for us both as well as a fun holiday home for the family. I did have to keep reminding myself this.

Every time we saw the family it was more poignant. Restrictions were ongoing so we weren't able to all get together however Boris Johnson the UK prime minister let everyone know we would be allowed to sociailise outdoors in groups of six but no more. Fortunately we were at that time a family of six.

Something I'd wanted to do ever since moving to Ferring seven years earlier was have a family picnic on the Green at Goring beach. Rock pooling and Rounders followed by lashings of ginger beer, that kind of thing. I was an avid Enid Blyton reader as a child. It may have taken seven years to actually get us all together to do this...oh I should explain to non UK readers...we not only had to co ordinate a day as we are a blended family. We also had to co ordinate with the weather! I was really looking forward to it and duly put in an early order for Marks and Spencer's delicious picnic food, just in case other people were thinking the same thing.

Then Rosa called to say that the appointment with the Notary was booked for the 1st October so we booked our flights to Italy for 26th September. As far as the house went viewings were still occurring even if sporadically and there was interest but no firm offer. The couple that had been interested still were. They however were waiting for an offer on their own house.

It was such a strange time almost limbo. There were or would be a multitude of loose ends to tie up but no firm knowledge of when we could or would go especially as the owner of the land was now expressing her sadness at the imminent sale. It had been in her family for generations and it was only because they now lived in a different region that they were selling. This made us feel uneasy in case she changed her mind. It was unlikely, as it was in writing meaning if she did pull out she would have to pay a heavy penalty but nothing about this time was reassuring.

We had daily updates of new covid cases resulting in new restrictions. We were days away from the Birthday picnic so pretty sure numbers wouldn't be altered before the 13th but what about travel? Would they stop flights again?

My 59th Birthday dawned warm and sunny to my intense relief. I was over the moon to have our little family all together for the first time since Christmas. Charlie and I arrived at the Goring Greensward first and set up the table and chairs. We weren't the only ones with the same thoughts in mind as dotted all around us were other groups of people, some far surpassing six. Goring Green is perfect for this kind of occasion. There are no parking restrictions kerbside so the only lugging to be done is across the green itself. We set up with the Tamarisk trees at our backs to shelter us if the wind changed. We had a large space around us for ball games. The beach itself was just past the trees. Pebbly at first but giving way to sand and rock pools as the tide went out.

I cannot express my joy when the kids arrived I am actually welling up as I type just with the pure emotional memory of that truly special day. It was perfect. One of those rare days in a persons life, any person anywhere in the world, where nothing went wrong. The sun continued to shine, the wind didn't whip up. The food went down a treat and we all laughed a lot. We played Boules and Rounders and just enjoyed being together all of us at last. If every day was like that I would certainly still be living in Ferring but life isn't like that. It simply can't be, because work, school and all the other commitments have to be seen to. Instead of bemoaning the fact that these fabulous times don't happen every week it is good to celebrate and treasure them when they do.

We all went down onto the beach and examined the rock pools spotting minuscule crabs and walking way out to the waters edge. By the end of the day we were all tired salty and happy. I can honestly say it was one of THE best days of my life.

Back to Italy

C hapter 20

On September 26th we flew into Romes Fumicino Airport. The covid cases were still on the increase. Zoe and Phoenix had come over to ours on the 20th I'd donned a hazmat suit with a mask and visor so that I could hug them both, and of course to make Peanut laugh. In all seriousness though we also didn't want to risk missing the Notary appointment.

By the 22nd the covid updates were saying people would be fined if they weren't wearing masks in public places so we had been anxiously watching for news on travel. Fortunately nothing had been said about it. Once again Karen, Rob and Ruby came to dog sit. And we were off.

At Rome airport we collected our hire car before driving across Italy to Pescara. Once again we turned right on to the Adriatica passing the bottom of 'Davids Mountain' and then past Vasto. We gave a cheer as we drove into Molise past it's big Benvenuto / Welcome sign. This trip we had booked into the hotel in San Martino itself. We had a lovely big balcony and after hot showers and a change of clothes were able to sit and enjoy the warmth of the late afternoon sun on our faces before walking over to Rosa's. We were very excited as a friend of Rosas had offered to design our house and be our Architect he was going to be there and show us his designs. Over the past weeks I had sent messages and drawings of my ideas, of the kind of house we would like to have, so we were eager to see his interpretations.

It was so good to see Mamma and Rosa, we are always made to feel so welcome, it's always a 'coming home' moment. However when I saw the drawings for the house my heart sank. It was nothing at all like we had said, or sketched out. Not at all and I was struggling not to let my feelings show whilst trying to find the words, the polite, nice kind words that is. So Charlie and I umm'd and mmm'd as we turned them this way and that both of us trying to no avail to figure out how on earth our simple design had become something slightly more futuristic.

We then all sat around the table to eat. While chewing my food my brain had been mulling over how to tell said person without being rude, and much more importantly to us, without causing any upset for Rosa. Somehow I found those words and with many apologies (I am English after all) managed to explain it wasn't as we had envisioned. With hindsight Charlie and I should have very politely said something along the lines of "its very kind of you but we feel we should wait before designing the house".

Something, anything along those lines but we didn't.

Hindsight is of course a wonderful thing.

Whirlwind.

Chapter 21

The next day saw us down on the land. Charlie had ordered a water testing kit back in the UK which had been delivered directly to Rosas house. He now set about lowering a plastic water bottle into the well. I was trying to work out the position where we would build the house bearing in mind that we wanted the view of the sea from the kitchen window I was trying to think my way around that while taking into account where the sun would come up and go down.

As it happens the position of the kitchen window is the only thing that really changed from my early sketches. It actually faces west where we now have a glorious view of the Mountains over in Abruzzo as we wash the dishes.

The land has sea views all the way along it's north side which are truly stunning however at that moment in time as I stood shading my eyes against the late September sunshine it wasn't possible to understand the full glory of this view because of the bamboo that grew at the very least to heights of 20 foot along the boundary line, along with huge clumps of brambles.

The Olive trees had all continued to be cared for and harvested over the years but a lot needed to be done peripherally.

With the water sitting in its little test bottles Charlie joined me as we examined the other trees, those, that is that weren't olives.

We found six plum trees on our side of the boundary, there was also another established plum tree not far from the little hut that stood on the brow of the rise. These huts are often made from stone, ours is brick. They have an open fireplace where the huge vats of tomatoes can be cooked for the sauce each year. Here too was the water tap that was essential for us to be able to live here in the fifth wheel while the house was being built. It is the law here in Italy that to legally live somewhere you must have running water and a source of electricity.

Next to the hut was a lovely, very large fig tree we picked some of it's fruit. This must surely be another sign as we hadn't eaten figs as delicious as these since being on the island of Paros with LouLou where we had stood around this huge old tree that belonged to her parents Jan and George in the garden of their Greek home.

Charlie, Zoe and me along with LouLou and her eldest son Marko had stood in a loose circle around this enormous Fig tree sucking the ripe fruit from skins that were still warm from the sun. I had never tasted fresh figs before and certainly never had figs as tasty since. That is until now.

Imagine then how happy I was to find a second fig tree nearby swiftly followed by the discovery of a third. All three were fully established I felt as though we'd found a treasure trove.

We also saw that there was a little pear tree, a couple of apples and a few Kaki trees. A Kaki is the Persimmon tree which at first neither of us especially liked until that is, we tasted a fully ripe fruit. Then we understood the attraction.

We'd spent a lovely couple of hours exploring the delights of what we hoped would soon be ours and excitedly told Mamma all about it over lunch with Rosa interpreting.

The following morning we had an appointment at the bank this was to give notice for the preparation of the cheques to give to the Notary on the 1st October. We had to have one cheque to pay the current owner, another to pay the Notary for his services and to pay taxes etc. Under Italian law you have to be able to fully understand everything that is being said. If you don't you have to nominate a representative who does. Rosa had kindly agreed to be our Representative so she would be signing the purchase documents in our name.

Everything was a whirlwind especially as the news was getting worse once again about covid cases and there were ominous talks of a second lockdown.

One day after reading more of this online Charlie and I had driven down to the land for another wander under the olive trees. Olive trees are so calming there is something very special about them, just coming here for half an hours respite from the whirlwind relaxed us and, reassured us. There is no doubt that we fully understood we were embarking upon a huge deal here.

After all, upping and leaving your home country, and your daughter is huge by itself, but doing so during a pandemic was even more so. Somehow though this all felt so absolutely right for us as a couple. It felt then as it still does now that we were somehow meant to come here, that it was our destiny.

I don't think I will ever completely feel at ease with myself for leaving Zoe in the UK even though she is in her thirties, and a Mum to three herself. But this is a mothers lot. We never stop thinking of and worrying about our children no matter how old they are they are always our children.

However I knew and still know that she doesn't need me to be living nearby. We both know that if she called I'd be on my way to her and she also knows she is and always will be my baby girl.

When Charlie and I were on the land among the olive trees any outside noise dissipated we were able to listen to our 'tummies' . (Listening to my tummy /solar plexus is something I always do and always have done when in any doubt. There are times when I don't listen and that is when problem's arise. I was listening. Right now I was fully tuned in and it was a definite 'go for it') We had to trust our gut instincts. That line... 'Feel the fear and do it anyway'... it encapsulates the whole thing.

We were fearful but we absolutely were going to do it anyway.

Land owners.

Chapter 22

The dream we'd first started talking about together around thirty years ago had just become a reality. We had signed and paid for two and a half acres (one hectare) of land.

Ok it was in a different country and it wasn't going to be a campsite but we had just become land owners.

Rosa was with us as our legal representative as well as friend and supporter. When we came out of the office we were greeted by Ann and David which was lovely. They'd driven over from Abruzzo to help us celebrate. Just along the road was a bar where we were able to sit in the sun and order a bottle of Prosecco. As the cork popped and the bubbles fizzed my feelings were as effervescent as the liquid pouring into our glasses. Charlie and I just gazed at each other.

We had done it.

I have to tell you that the actual process of signing wasn't without it's own tensions so it wasn't until we'd walked out of sight of the

Notaries office that the pair of us had a moment to even begin to process the fact that Casa Phoenix was ours.

Charlie and I had followed Rosas car to Larino. Larino is just a twenty minute drive from SMIP and as lovely as the scenery is I wasn't taking any of it in. I was feeling far too anxious. We'd heard that the seller was feeling upset about selling the land it having been, (I believe) in her family for a couple of hundred years and it was only due to the logistics of living in a different region that it had been on the market in the first place.

She was apparently still upset and now that we were just ten minutes away from the office instead of drinking in the views I was imagining scenarios where she didn't turn up, or at the point of signing refused or...

But then we turned into the street and parked. Whew, the seller was standing outside with her husband. We all shook hands and proceeded into the office donning our masks as we did so. They were a pleasant couple and Rosa made small talk with them while Charlie and I tried to follow the conversation. However when the Notary called us in the poor lady started to show signs of distress and I, feeling dreadful for her asked Rosa to translate and tell her that we would look after the land and the trees.

In we went with our masked faces. Charlie and I signed the piece of paper that gave Rosa the authority to sign on our behalf following which we sat quietly out of the way while the owner, her husband and Rosa signed everything. We also agreed that even though the land would be legally ours by the time it came to harvest that they could have this years olive crop. I asked if we could just have a bottle of the olive oil. Before we knew it we were handing over the cheques and shaking hands. The sellers walked out first, the Notary wished us well and we followed them. There was no moment however to even exchange smiles because a piercing sound of weeping and wailing assailed us. We couldn't possibly ignore it. The poor lady was distraught, her husband was trying to comfort her to no avail. Again Rosa translated for us as I tried to assure her that we hadn't just bought the land to visit once in a while but that we intended to live there and nurture the trees that had been so well cared for by her and her family for so many years.

I have to admit that after this continued for a while longer before we'd even left the office, only to resume as soon as we had all stepped outside, my empathy was starting to strain.

We had spotted David and Ann and were wanting to go and greet them especially as they had driven for an hour and a half just to be with us on this momentous occasion. However, I couldn't just walk off and leave this poor woman crying. Eventually to my relief her husband led her away to their car.

While understanding the emotions of handing over something of such familial and historical value to her I also felt rather exasperated by the time we'd walked away.

Now, at last sitting with Rosa, David and Ann it slowly started to sink in. Smiling broadly we raised our glasses to "Casa Phoenix".

A Brilliant Idea

*C*hapter 23

That night we celebrated at the Agriturismo. The pizza restaurant which is just outside the town of San Martino itself. We had a long table of eleven. It was very merry and Charlie and I were so relieved. It was done. All the tensions of - Would we be able to fly to Italy? - Would travel restrictions come back into play? - Would the Notaries office remain open? - Would restrictions come back in? - Would the seller change her mind?

All of this fell away amidst the congratulations and laughter. Of course new tensions and fears would soon sprout up again but they were going to wait until the following morning.

It was now October the 2nd 2020, we were due to fly home the following day so it made sense to spend some time on the land. This was the first time we'd come down since it became officially ours and of course it felt different.

This was going to be our home. Pinch me, this beautiful place now belonged to us. As we stood there under the gentle whisper of the olive leaves I turned to Charlie

" I think we need to get out here as quickly as possible"

The murmurs of another lockdown were getting louder by the day

"What do you think?"

He agreed. However the logistics of it all seemed a high mountain to climb. Then I had one of those lightbulb moments that occur once in a blue moon

"Oh my God I've just thought of something"

Charlie was looking at me in an 'Uh Oh what now' kind of way. After over thirty years together he's more than used to my loud excited outbursts but what on earth could I have thought of to do with this current situation. I continued

" Of course they may not be interested but we could ask couldn't we?"

"Ask what and who?"

As we often finish each others sentences and seem to be on each others wave lengths much more than not I was a little surprised that he didn't know exactly what I was talking about.

" Karen and Rob " I exclaimed.

Around a year before our 'besties', friends Karen and Rob had decided that as soon as Rob retired they would go travelling for a year or so. They were going to go full time in their motorhome spending a few months exploring an area in Europe then back to the UK and drive up to Scotland before taking a trip to another part of Europe. It was a great idea and they were both very excited. One of their daughters and her husband moved into Karen and Robs house and let their own smaller property to tenants.

Their first trip was to France then into Spain. They were actually still in Spain in November 2019 about to head home for Christmas even as we ourselves were driving home from our stay in Abruzzo. They had then had a stay in the south-west of England, we'd even met up for a weekend near Bristol. Unfortunately that was to be the last of their jaunts as covid was about to upset the apple cart.

They had spent the first lockdown on the driveway of their home. A far cry from the imagined winter months in the warmth of somewhere like the south of France. Instead they found themselves almost on a traffic island due to the road network around the house. Now, with the imminent likelihood of a second lockdown my lightbulb moment burst into play.

"So what do you think?"

Charlie thought for barely a moment before replying that if they would it could be a brilliant solution. Back at the hotel I sent them a text along the lines of

" We've got an idea. Not sure if you guys would be interested … if you are though it could be a great solution for us both…What would you think of the idea of moving into our place to oversee Viewings and look after the house? It would enable us to drive out here before we're all banned from travelling anywhere. Plus it would mean we could be here before the Brexit implications"… PING.

Followed swiftly by "You would be back in a house during the next lockdown and we would relax knowing our house isn't empty" …PING.

I don't quite know how things would have turned out if they hadn't responded in the way that they did but thankfully they said Yes.

This time when we left San Martino we did so in the expectation of returning within a few weeks. We left early in the morning so we could have a leisurely drive to Rome.

At Rome airport they had what I can only describe as Heat Sensory machines. Basically they could tell if someone was running a fever. We didn't feel as though we were and didn't feel unwell however, the mere sight of it made me feel nervous. The thought of being in quarantine right then with so much to be done as well as having to return to Italy before the Brexit cut off date was mind boggling. I'm surprised my temperature didn't go off the scale just because of the scenario that was playing out in my head as we got closer and closer to the machine and the security person sitting at a desk beside it scanning a monitor. I felt a huge wave of relief as we were both gestured onwards.

When we returned to Ferring Karen and Rob were there to greet us and we sat discussing the logistics of my idea over a meal that Karen had thoughtfully and tastily prepared. It was such a relief and also exciting that they were on board.

As we had already started getting things in motion with an International removal company we could now fix a date with them. We needed also to sort things out about the house sale. Thankfully our excellent solicitor Moira McFarlane is also a good friend and she made it all far easier for us than it would have been with a stranger especially with all the covid restrictions. Karen and Rob had no timelines to worry about as they were living in their home on wheels and would simply drive the 15 miles or so to our place.

What Charlie and I needed to do was pack everything into boxes, decide what would go to Italy and what could be sold or donated.

Also there were last minute health checks making sure Tetanus jabs were up to date and enough medication, for me until I found a Rheumatoid Consultant. Months before at the outset I had checked that I would be able to get my medication and to double check on that information I had contacted the British Embassy in Rome. They were very helpful and replied quickly that yes I would be able to.

Our Hot Tub was barely a year old and a very good one so we offered to sell it back to the company we'd bought it from. However the pitiful thousand pound that they offered was laughable so we gave it to Zoe and Cyrus. We are both so happy that we did as they all use it all the time.

Of course looming ever nearer was the moment we would have to say goodbye to the kids and I was dreading it. Once again I was going through all those guilt ridden thoughts and feelings about leaving them. I have to say as I am writing this, that as hard and soul wrenching as it was to leave them, and it was. I do know that for Charlie and I as people in our own right it was absolutely the best decision and aside from missing them we are living our best and happiest lives.

We have no regrets. We love our life here despite all the ups and downs of living in the caravan for three years, the build and in recent months all the money worries as everything ended up costing a lot more than we originally thought. That part of it has been a horrible strain but living here is still a dream come true.

I just hope with all my heart that they are all going to love it when they come and it will be the start of them coming regularly.

The boxes were by now piling up in every room. Every piece of furniture either had a sticker on it scrawled with 'Urben-Italy' or was in the Donate pile. By now my lovely neat packing had started to evolve into frantic pushing and squeezing things into the corners of boxes. I had to write on each box as the removals company needed a list of everything to go through customs. Karen and Rob came over and helped us. Rob climbed up into the attic and made sure it was empty of our belongings and swept clean of dust and debris. They were stars. The house was no longer feeling like our comfortable home especially as every personal item was now either in a box or, in the van. I knew that as we would be in the van for around a year, maybe a year and a half, I would need lots of personal things especially framed photos of the kids. Little did I know that we were going to be living in that van for 3 years

Where Oil paintings had hung there were now only slightly brighter patches of wall. Then of course there was the garden, a nightmare in itself with pots and tables, garden ornaments and our Pizza oven. That was definitely coming with us. We'd bought it a few years before and all of us loved it. Many a get together and party had been based around it.

On Charlies 60 th Birthday I'd made balls and balls of pizza dough and sauce for the topping. Zoe must have made up at least 20 pizzas to order with her Dad cooking them in the oven before guests started making up their own second helpings. That was such a lovely memory that party. Phoenix had sung 'Happy Birthday' to her Pops with the karaoke microphone. Then she'd sung again because I hadn't switched the phones camera to video in time to capture it.

Zoe and Cyrus organised a crane to come over and hoist the hot tub up and over the roof. I felt immensely grateful that it was a bungalow as I gazed upward nervously wondering how on earth they were going to avoid the stainless steel chimney from the Wood burner. Thankfully it went up and over with no mishaps. Everywhere looked empty and sad and quite honestly if it wasn't for the imminent big goodbye I sometimes felt I'd love to just flee it all. We fell into bed each night worn out. Instead of my usual bedtime reading matter I was looking through lists and ticking things off. I'd still be checking those lists while Charlie had dropped off to sleep. The dogs too were a little anxious sensing something was happening and hoping they weren't being left behind again. As much as they enjoyed having Karen, Rob and Ruby staying with them they obviously preferred to be with Mum and Dad. I think they felt reassured when they came onto the van as I was putting their doughnut beds onboard along with a basket of their toys.

We had slowly been saying goodbye to other friends over these couple of weeks. Elizabeth and Tracey invited us down for a delicious meal. It was a lovely evening with Betsy and Archie able to say their own goodbyes to their Yorkshire terriers Olive and Teddy.

Sue, Charlies sister and her partner came down to say their goodbyes and then it was the dreaded moment.

Broken

*C*hapter 24

That's how my heart felt. Completely broken, not in two but into a thousand pieces. What the blooming heck was I doing? What were WE doing?

Saying goodbye to them was THE hardest thing. They all came over, and saying goodbye to the four of them was awful. It was hard enough with Cyrus and Naz but they weren't as emotional about it as my two girls. Oh my God it was terrible. Phoenix was in bits. I tried so hard not to fall apart but the worse part was when Zoe cried. She like me had been keeping it together but when she let go I was in pieces. Waving them off as we had done from that same spot in the road so many times over the past seven years knowing this was now the last time from Shell Cottage.

I could barely see but kept waving and waving.

Charlie and I were by now completely exhausted. We had already felt physically and mentally wrought but now emotionally it was all such a lot. We were snapping and snarling at each other at any given opportunity I was constantly on the verge of tears and felt so ripped apart from saying goodbye to the kids that this behaviour we were both guilty of, made everything worse. It made it even more difficult because we have never in over 30 years been like that with each other. Oh, we bicker and pull faces at each other, sometimes we're like little kids ourselves. We've also had the odd screaming match, show me a couple that never has over three decades. But this, this wasn't us at all and it made everything so much more difficult. My stomach felt as though it was in knots I mean how could I have said goodbye to Zoe, to my loved ones to go and live in a different country with this sniping snarling pig? Of course we both said sorry to each other, we hugged. Then I cried some more and probably asked him why he was being such a pig but then had to laugh because obviously I'd been a grunting sow.

I honestly don't think we could have done any of this if we hadn't been such good friends as well as lovers. The fact that we can always talk things out and end up laughing has always stood us in good stead. We've certainly been thankful for that over the past three years.

As broken as I felt by saying goodbye to the kids I knew, that is I knew once I'd calmed down a bit, that as hard as this was, it really was the right thing for us.

Being a parent isn't something that you do for a few years being a parent is forever. That doesn't mean that you have to lose your own personality and life. Zoe is a strong and independent young woman with her own family and business but she knows that whenever she wants either me or her Dad we'll be there for her.

Mad Dash

*C*hapter 25

I stood and looked around at what had been our home for the past seven years, it no longer felt like ours. In each corner of every room stood boxes. The majority of them were stacked into the second bedroom. I certainly wasn't feeling anything like the wrench that I had when we had left our family home in Patcham. Then I had felt so sad at leaving. I hadn't even wanted to leave it. It's four walls had just seemed to pulsate with all the happy memories of Zoe growing up and then of Phoenix being there as a tiny baby then as a toddler, on sleepovers. Of all the family meals and get togethers. Christmas mornings where I would set the scene the night before and on Christmas morning itself after all of us including the dogs had opened our stockings while piled onto our bed. Charlie and I would go into the sitting room where he would get the Wood burner going brightly. I'd make the coffee (for us) and hot chocolate (for Zoe), the breakfast table I'd laid the night before with Christmas crockery but I still had the fairy lights to turn on and a Christmas CD set to play. Then, as he did every year Charlie would groan as I insisted we join Zoe in the hallway where she had been patiently waiting with the dogs. I'd shut the door behind us. By now Charlie would be loudly grumbling "Do we have to do this every year?" But it was said half heartedly as if expected of him because somehow the real magic of Christmas was when Zoe slowly opened the sitting room door. We would stand behind her and there was the room totally transformed from any ordinary morning into a winter wonderland. The Christmas tree lights twinkling, Bing Crosby crooning, intriguing presents under the branches and a suspiciously Dad sized boot print in the sprinkled 'snow' nearby. These memories and many more had been going through my head when we'd left Patcham. I'd cried most of the drive from Brighton to Ferring but now, well now I was almost eager to just go. The hardest and most awful part had been the goodbyes but the house was just a house and we would be taking all the memories with us.

Everything that we thought we might need for a year in the caravan was packed into the Fifth wheel and also into every nook and cranny of the truck. If we got pulled over and weighed goodness only knows what would happen we had so much stuff. The reality was that ready or not if we were going to do this we had to do it now we couldn't hang about because everything was pointing to an imminent second lock down which would mean not being allowed into Italy and not becoming Residents before the end of 2020.

We had made our decision, made our heart wrenching farewells now we just needed to get on with it.

Karen and Rob arrived with Ruby around four in the afternoon I think it's fair to say that they must've been looking forward to being in a house again even if it was in a state of flux. We in turn were so happy knowing that we weren't going off and leaving it empty. We sat and went through all the bits and pieces like where the stopcock is , the estate agents numbers etc. We then ate a last meal together in the kitchen before lots of hugs goodbye then we were climbing up into the truck and were away waving out of the windows until we turned the corner and they were out of sight.

I still felt discombobulated. We were still snapping and snarling at each other. I felt pretty miserable especially as we drove past Brighton on the way to Newhaven. I wanted so much to go and hug Zoe, Cyrus, Pea and Naz.

Did I really want to leave at all? In fact...why was I ?

We didn't speak much on that short drive. We were both exhausted emotionally and physically. I knew that as much as we felt at odds it was only because we were so drained. I snuck my hand slowly over to rest it on his thigh and he slid one hand off the wheel and held onto mine. We were ok. We would be ok.

It would all be ok.

On our way

*C*hapter 26

We arrived in France at 5am it was pouring with rain and still dark. Off the ferry we went into the driving rain with the windscreen wipers sweeping back and forth at full speed. Just out of Dieppe we pulled into the first parking lay-by we came to. The dogs quickly had their wee's as the rain was hammering down even harder now and they wanted to be out of it just as much as we did. We all four of us stepped up into the Fifth wheel and crawled onto the bed falling asleep immediately.

We woke around 11.00 and the sky, although still watery was at least brighter than it had been at 5.30 that morning. We were all curled up together in what felt like a cave as we hadn't been able to extend the slide outs so had literally taken the two steps into the bedroom, climbed onto the bed and zonked out. So the first morning of our new life was in said lay-by drinking mugs of coffee sitting up in bed as believe me you couldn't get further than the little kitchen area.

Thankfully as coffee is always high on our list of priorities we had stored the kettle, coffee and a Cafetiere in a spot that was always going to be easy to reach.

This is perhaps a good point at which to describe the layout of the Fifth wheel. If you, the reader have never been on or inside a fifth wheel you may be imagining that we had lots of space and comfort at each stop that we made. When parked up ready for habitation with all four slide outs extended the space is great. This is ours...

The entrance is approximately the middle of van, walk up a couple of steps and in through the front door. Immediately in front of you is a kitchen with a window, there is a corner sink set in a worktop which goes to the right, to the left is a gas cooker which has a decent sized oven and four gas rings on the stove top. A microwave sits above the cooker and there is a reasonable amount of storage, actually its a good amount of storage for holidays however for full-time living it becomes a challenge that was ours yet to discover. To the left of the kitchen is a sitting room with a dining space. A lovely large window across the back wall in front of which is a tv and below that a faux electric log fire. To the left of this window is a two seater sofa that becomes a double bed, opposite in the other slide out our dining table and two chairs. There was also a leather reclining chair. It was all a little dark which isn't to our taste so we had lots of pale throws and cushions to lighten it. It also has tinted windows which I grew to both love and hate. Love because they helped against the glare and heat of the sun especially during August and hate, because everything felt dark and gloomy. Again when just for a holiday it was fine however in the winter months when you want as much light as possible it's not so nice.

There is a good sized fridge freezer which stands between the sofa and the front door. Walking past the front door and up two steps there is a door on your left which leads to the bathroom here there is a walk in shower, loo and a sink. Out of there, turn left and you're in the bedroom. This is a great size for a holiday boasting a double bed with a bedside table and little window each side of it, a fitted wardrobe with glass doors along the back wall and a dressing table at the foot of the bed with another window. We were really happy to have this as our home for a year or so. Its the size of a small one room flat. However, when you are travelling, parking up just for a night and you have it packed full to bursting with goodness knows what, unable to extend the slide-outs then it is a very different story. With both the living area slide-outs locked into travelling position and every inch of space stuffed with something its just impossible to get inside. The fridge doesn't slide out so that is always accessible as is the kitchen but even that area had bags and boxes everywhere. We also needed to take into consideration anything heavy had to be stored low down so floor space was limited. As for the bedroom, that too has a double slide. When locked into a closed position the bed touches the dressing table and the side windows disappear. Again we had bags and boxes crammed into every available space.

So yes it did feel as if we were sitting up in a little cave with that morning coffee.

Whilst on the boat we'd both calmed down from the stress of the last few days and were once again best mates, no longer sniping at each other. In fact now that we were on the other side of the channel, the commitment well and truly made (as if it hadn't been when we signed and paid for the land) we both felt a sense of peace.

We were now looking forward.

Two things preoccupied us most. Firstly the real possibility of getting pulled over onto a weigh bridge we didn't even want to imagine what would have to be thrown out! If you are pulled over and found to be over weight anything over and above has to be off loaded then and there. Scary thought!

Then there was the whole Covid uncertainty. Nothing was clear. We knew the next lockdown was imminent and had read we would have to take tests when we entered Italy. However what we didn't know was how, where or when. Were there going to be testing areas at the border? For all we knew people in hazmat suits and masks could be waiting at the entry points for travellers. As we'd left the UK we had had to fill in 'Self Declaration Forms' to say we weren't unwell and that we hadn't been in contact with anyone who had been unwell it was all a little strange. A kind of limbo.

The drive was pretty uneventful except for when we found ourselves at Versailles. How we took the route through Paris we don't know it certainly wasn't the plan and how we found ourselves at Versailles was even stranger. But there we were trundling along the road having followed the Sat Nav's advice and taking the left turn at a roundabout.

"Oh my giddy aunt" I declared "Look, its Versailles"

Charlie was absolutely not looking at the Palace in all it's glory he was swearing at the Sat Nav and trying to manoeuvre us out of a Strictly No Caravan zone. Thankfully the street was pretty empty due no doubt to the covid situation but I was gleefully drinking it in. Never having visited Versailles but having read so many books about it I was ok with the Sat Nav for this particular mistake. On the other hand Charlie was very rude to it as he manoeuvred us out of the situation. At least we didn't get stopped. That didn't bear thinking about. We made it to Dijon, Burgundy on the Wednesday night and managed to call Zoe as we had at last got wifi. We were also able to get the slide outs extended so had some comfort which we needed, especially Charlie after all the driving.

Italy

*C*hapter 27

We came across Mont Blanc with the Sat Nav once again trying to take us all over the place, this time though it wasn't funny but actually a little scary. With at least 12 metres length of caravan and truck combined the last thing we wanted was another Lake Como situation on top of a snowy mountain.

While trying to navigate the actual navigation system we were also wondering what lay in wait for us at the border. I cannot stress enough what a strange time it was in 2020. Our generation had never known anything like it before. It was as though one of the blockbuster Apocalypse films had come to life. Lock-downs. Health tests. Lists of deaths. Lists of infections. The television and internet were full of it. It was a time of intense anxiety for everybody.

Which is why we had no idea what to expect as we approached the Italian border

Italy had been devastated by the virus early on with so many deaths that it would be understandable if they had tough restrictions on entry so we approached with trepidation.

Would we even be allowed in?

Talk about anti climatic. Nobody in hazmat suits or otherwise. No signs of a testing area. In fact we didn't see anyone at all. It was as if covid didn't exist. On we drove. We were here. We were in Italy at last we could breathe.

Charlie drove for ten hours stopping for lunch and a rest on the bed. After the brief nap we continued until we reached Modena and found the Camper-stop that David had told us about. It was just right for a stopover we were able to pull into a space and let the dogs stretch their legs and do their ablutions. We humans too were in need of some leg stretching especially Charlie. It had been a long haul but here we were in Italy. We hadn't been turned away at the border and having spoken to David and Ann who reassured us that they would take us to a hospital near them for testing within the time limit set by the government we could at last start to relax.

Once again we all squeezed into the bedroom. I had heated some baked beans which we ate on buttery toast perched on the edge of the bed with our feet balancing on the bags and boxes. Betsy and Archie had eaten and had already found their spaces on the bed. Noses and paws twitching they were in a deep sleep no doubt dreaming of the Italian rabbits they'd sniffed as we had walked around the parking area. It wasn't long before we crashed out too.

We arrived at Casa Mae by four o'clock the next afternoon. Exhausted, and relieved. No hugs this time just big smiles and elbow nudges as we were all being virus aware. Charlie drove into the same spot as the year before. We connected the electricity and the gas and filled up with water. The dogs were over the moon, free to run around again and to be reunited with their cousins.

First thing I did was to let Zoe know we were there safely.

Second thing was a shower. I stood under the hot water not knowing whether to laugh or cry. I think I did both.

It was Friday the 23 rd October was it real? It didn't seem real, far from it. It was only 22 days ago that we had signed for, bought and paid for the land. Packed up our British lives, part of which we'd trundled across France into Italy like a giant snail, our temporary home attached to our backs.

What the heck had we done!

Covid tests

Chapter 28

Although we'd slept really well we woke up still feeling exhausted, not just physically but also mentally drained. It had all been a lot and we had to catch up with ourselves. Casa Mae was the perfect place to do that. The van door opened onto a stunning vista across the valley, the sun was warm. We couldn't go anywhere or do anything. We were now in quarantine. It was a buffer between our old life in Ferring and our new one in San Martino. Both David and Ann were great I think they could see how shattered we were and they themselves had of course done this huge move so understood more than most.

I pottered around the van arranging a few bits and pieces now that we'd extended the slide-outs. I didn't do too much as we would be driving to Molise in a few days but we did need some space to move around in. Ann prepared a delicious Roast for us all on the Sunday and we were able to eat outside in the warmth of the sun.

The following morning we tried to sort out our covid tests. David took us to the hospital at Atessa, then to his Doctor but we couldn't get one at either place so we called Rosa who in turn called the hospitals at Gizzi and Atessa. We were to go to Gizzi the following morning for 8.00. So we could now relax, we knew what we would be doing and were doing everything we could to keep to the government's guide lines.

Around one in the morning I was woken by something crawling on my face I must have sleepily cupped it and thrown it down the bed initially thinking nothing more until this sharp stinging pain started just under my eye on the socket bone. I thought I'd scratched myself but literally by the second it worsened. Climbing out of bed I went to splash water on it but to my horror when I glanced in the bathroom mirror the area around my eye was swelling and it really hurt. Charlie who had been in a deep sleep until the bright light penetrated it groggily asked if I was ok. When I told him something had been crawling on me he looked in the bed and there it was, a spider. It was caught in the crochet of the beautiful throw that Sue, Charlies sister had made us as a farewell gift. He gently and warily extricated it and put it into a glass. The pain was really starting to bother me and we didn't have any cortisone. We'd packed a kitchen sink but not that. Pulling on some clothes we went to knock on David and Anns front door. Thankfully Ann had some and gently applied it to my swollen face, we then trundled back to bed full of apologies for waking them.

The next day the area around the bite was really swollen. Along with a deep throbbing ache. Laying in bed gazing at the empty spot next to the little window I realised the culprit must have been the spider that had been sitting there for the last couple of days. I'd seen it but thought nothing of it. Never having had a fear of spiders it hadn't bothered me. Now if I see one I gently remove it, or I ask Charlie to.

They may catch mosquitoes and flies but I never want another bite like that. Especially after I had googled it and discovered it was a Fake Black Widow in fact, it was a Noble false widow. Easily identified once you know because the markings on its back look like a skull. Although not deadly the bite can vary from a wasp like sting to excruciating pain. Unfortunately my experience was the latter and the swelling took at least a week to go down. No spiders were hurt during all of this as after I'd travelled to Gizzi with it and tried to show the chemist what had bitten me I took it to the very end of Davids long driveway and let it out.

The hospital at Gizzi had a queue of cars being slowly directed towards the testing area. Everyone was in masks and it all seemed strange after days of seeing hardly anyone at all. At Casa Mae we were in a beautiful bubble surrounded by countryside and birds whilst there covid seemed to be a bad dream. Yet here we were once again seeing the effects of this virus. When it was our turn it was a little difficult making ourselves understood as our Italian was virtually non existent in this context and they didn't speak English however once we told them our Codice Fiscale which is the tax code that we'd obtained back in August everything went smoothly. This was the first time we'd had an official test and it did feel strange having a masked and gloved person sticking a giant cotton wool bud up each nostril and another around the inside of our mouths. We were handed pieces of paper with a number on and handing over our phone numbers were told we would get the results in two days. Next stop was the chemist where when I tried to show the pharmacist the spider which I must add was safely in the jar. Screaming she jumped back two paces and waved her arms about. Ok all well and good, but what about this pointing to my swollen throbbing face. Shouting at me just to ensure I understood she pointed out of the window "Ospedale". We went back to the hospital. "No, you can't come in here. Only covid tests or covid admissions". Back we went to the chemist where with no spider on view she was calm enough to point out the cortisone.

So now we had had our tests, we had fulfilled our legal and moral obligations.

On the Wednesday I stayed in Casalanguida with the dogs while Ann, David and Charlie drove over to San Martino as they wouldn't be seeing anyone it seemed ok to do that. They went armed with various tools needed to trim the branches so that we would be able to drive LouLou Bella (LouLou Bella 2) onto the land and park her up. They did a great job of it along with the house sign and post box concreted into position. Ann took lots of photos to show me. It felt good seeing our 'Casa Phoenix' sign there at the entrance. I sent the photos to Zoe.

Covid restrictions were hotting up again here in Italy and we were starting to get nervous about being stuck in Abruzzo as a travel ban between the regions was on the agenda. There was also another reason, this was down to the weather. It had rained on Wednesday night which made Charlie feel nervous about how muddy it could get, after all it was now the end of October if it rained again would we even be able to drive up to the area we had designated for ourselves. Although we still hadn't had our results by Thursday we made the decision to drive over on the Friday morning. We weren't going to stop anywhere we would simply be driving from A to B and stay there until our results came back. Ann went shopping and got us some provisions so we were all stocked up for the foreseeable. On Friday morning we said goodbye to them both, gave Harvey and JD extra hugs as we couldn't hug the humans and off we went.

The sun was shining as we passed the big MOLISE sign and we felt like we'd come home. We drove up to San Martino through the little town of Portocannone with our home from home on our backs. We were now in familiar territory and as we passed the sign that declared Comune of San Martino in Pensilis we started to look out for the Casa Phoenix sign and there it was. It glittered in the sunshine welcoming us to our new home. I heard Charlies sharp intake of breath as he indicated left, he didn't want to slow down to a halt because if it had rained over here he wanted a bit of traction. Luckily the road behind and in front was clear he turned the steering wheel accelerated slightly and pulled off the road. Nothing impeded us as we sailed on up the incline. With a bit of too-ing and fro-ing we backed up and he turned off the engine. We had really and truly arrived.

Home sweet home

Chapter 29

Calm descended. At that moment we knew that despite all the anxiety despite the goodbyes and heart ache we were where we were meant to be. It's strange to say but it truly is as though it was written in our stars to come here. Of course we could have decided that it was too much of a gamble, we had certainly felt fearful, but somehow a whole load of little twists and turns steered us here and, equally somehow we had both followed the path.

I kept thinking of Doreen, Charlies mum. If it hadn't been for her we wouldn't have been able to purchase the land. Charlie too was thinking of her and had been to have a private word with her, we both felt thankful.

Betsy and Archie were very excited as we walked them all around. Starting at the North side where they met our neighbours German shepherd down to the back entrance, then back up past all the 20 foot high bamboo which creaked ominously in the breeze back we went to LouLou Bella ll which now had her steps down and all 4 slide outs extended. Both dogs were a little frustrated at being on long leads which were staked into the ground whenever we weren't all on a walk. They soon discovered they could still chase the sunning green lizards who hadn't yet realised there were interlopers.

At last we could unpack and unload. Out came the picnic table and chairs which we set up under the nearest olive tree. I picked the last of the fruit left on the Fig trees which we ate with bread, cheese and tomatoes. Have you ever eaten ripe Italian tomatoes in Italy? If you haven't you are in for a treat when you do. If you have and you're reading this anywhere but Italy I bet your mouth is watering. I remember exactly where I ate my first tomato in Italy. It was in Rome at a cafe near the bottom of the Spanish Steps when Zoe took me for my birthday. We had ordered a Caprese Salad which, when I bit into the thick slice of red flesh I felt as though I'd entered culinary heaven. It was an explosion like no other so when I say our first meal was cheese and tomatoes with fresh bread and figs it may sound a little lack lustre but hell no, it was heavenly. Then there were the views, I glance up from the keyboard right now and I am looking at the same view. We built our house on the very spot where we ate that first lunch. We are still wowed by this view each and every day.

We had a generator for temporary power until we could arrange for an electricity supply. We had the water tap just outside the little hut so we didn't have to worry about that. It felt good to put everything away. I was able to hang our clothes in the wardrobe. I loved being able to place the framed photos of everyone around the room. I put a vase of flowers on the cabinet next to the tv along with scented candles. A bowl of fruit on the little dining table and books on shelves. It was beginning to look like home.

That first evening we sat outside gazing at the blanket of stars sipping red wine until we realised just how sleepy we were. We slept so well that night.

Pizza and Prosecco

Chapter 30

It was Halloween the 31st October. We had our test results, they were negative so we were no longer in quarantine. After breakfast we decided to clear out the little hut which we call the Rustic. Once it was swept clean we could padlock the door and keep tools and the like inside. We had crammed not only household goods inside the truck and the van but also all kinds of tools and implements.

You'll see these huts all over Italy they are not only used for storage and shelter from the weather but also boast a large stone fireplace this is often used to cook the tomato sauce in the huge batches that once bottled see the family through until the following summer. I would imagine it is also put in use during the olive harvest for warmth on a chilly November morning and to cook one of the large tasty local sausages in the hot embers.

Collecting up everything that remained within Charlie jumped as a large scorpion scuttled across the wall. I was a little nervous after that and even more so when Charlie found a snake skin. It was huge I hate to imagine how big the actual snake was, thankfully if it had still been around the noise of us sent it slithering else where. An old jacket revealed itself as a home, indeed a nest for a plethora of baby geckos which we gently laid out so they could stay or go as they pleased. Another scorpion didn't like the disturbance and disappeared into a large crack in the wall. There were also lots of lizards both green and brown varieties. Zoe, Charlie and I have called them 'Billy bobs' ever since our first visit to the island of Paros so they always make us smile. Then there was an egg, come to think of it why didn't the snake eat the egg? Probably because it knew it wasn't fresh which we found out when it exploded at the touch of the brooms bristles it STUNK. Aside from the wildlife there were cups, glasses and old tools. We kept it all as it was the history of the place. I washed the glasses and cups and stored them in a corner. Charlie dusted off the tools and hung them on the wall. We had a clean bare hut ready for storage.

The most important thing to do was to fence in an area around the van so that the dogs were safe. Although the road isn't busy in comparison to a major town it is busy at certain times, like lunch time when everyone heads home for pasta, they also tend to drive rather fast. Now we were out of quarantine we were able to go into the Builders Merchants just along the road where we bought our materials.

With Fifty metres of fencing we were able to create a garden area, the dogs were now able to roam inside the fence line. There was plenty of space to have the table and chairs outside too and Charlie fashioned together a little gate. We had untangled our solar lights (which was no mean feat) and hung them in various trees. Then I went indoors and made apple sponge pudding and custard for the little festa or party we had planned for that evening. Meanwhile Charlie made a small fire pit with some large stones he had found by the well.

That evening Rosa and Mamma came down to officially welcome us to San Martino. They brought with them freshly cooked Pizzas from one of the Pizzerias in town along with an ice cold bottle of Prosecco. There was a full moon which lit up the Olive Grove, our solar lights twinkled in the trees. The low fire crackled in the pit and we were pleasantly full. The Prosecco sparkled 'Salute' we cheered.

"Benvenuto a San Martino " said Mamma.

End of Book 1.

Afterword

Thank you so very much to **Robert Norfolk** especially for your invaluable pointers, and **Lindsay Hartley Russell** for also reading through the entire book for me. Grazie mille **Alissa Frame** who while staying with us listened to me read each and every chapter giving such positive and helpful feedback. (Listening with Mother)

Melissa Hull at **DIGITAL MOLISE info@digitalmolise.com** What can I say except heartfelt Grazie... Grazie...Grazie. Your knowledge and assistance around everything IT has been invaluable.

Nathan Heinrich The amazing wonderful host of the **'I Moved to Italy' Podcast.** Thank you so much for your generous Foreword. Fates aligned when we met.

And a huge **THANK YOU** to each and every one of you who reads my book. I can't believe it. I actually wrote and published one! It's a dream come true.

I have a blog at **www.movingtomolise.com** please head over there and leave me a message & If you would like to experience the beauty of our Olive Grove our B&B website is: **www.casa-phoenix.com**

Look out for the second book in the series...Coming around Christmas time.

Living the Italian Dream Book 2: Moving to Molise

Join Karren and Charlie as they navigate becoming Residents in their new town. Charlie has to have an emergency surgery. The joy of when two new additions arrive in the family. It's their first Olive Harvest...and Karren goes back to school.

That's just some of what's to come in Book 2 in the series of:

LIVING THE ITALIAN DREAM

Ciao for now X

Printed in Great Britain
by Amazon